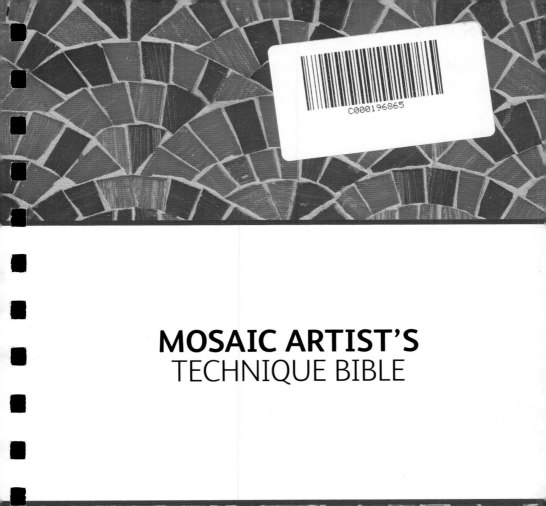

MOSAIC ARTIST'S
TECHNIQUE BIBLE

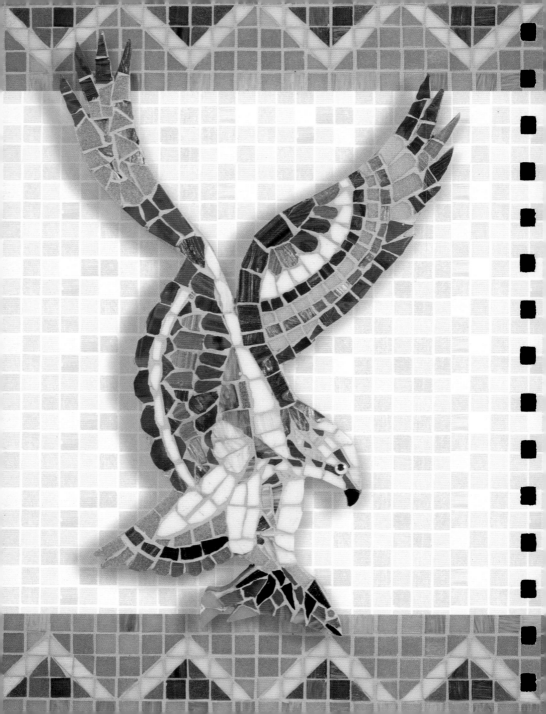

MOSAIC ARTIST'S
TECHNIQUE BIBLE

A STEP-BY-STEP GUIDE

TERESA MILLS

APPLE

A QUARTO BOOK

First published in the UK in 2009 by
Apple Press
7 Greenland Street
London NW1 0ND
United Kingdom
www.apple-press.com

ISBN: 978-1-84543-281-2

QUAR.MATB

Conceived, designed and produced by
Quarto Publishing plc
The Old Brewery
6 Blundell Street
London
N7 9BH

Senior editor: Lindsay Kaubi
Copy editor: Liz Dalby
Art director: Caroline Guest
Art editor: Emma Clayton
Designer: Karin Skånberg
Photographer: Martin Norris
Illustrator: John Woodcock

Creative director: Moira Clinch
Publisher: Paul Carslake

Colour separation by Modern Age Repro·
House Ltd, Hong Kong
Manufactured in China by Midas Printing
International Ltd

1 3 5 7 9 10 8 6 4 2

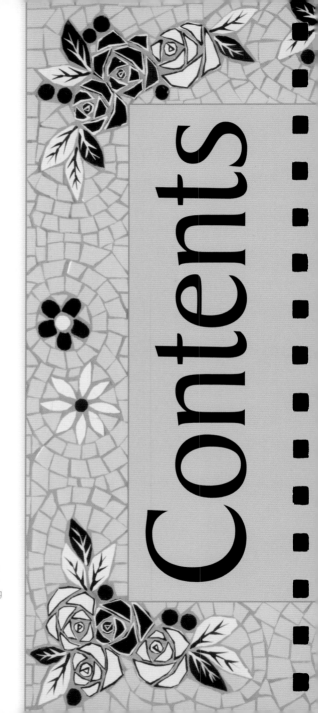

Contents

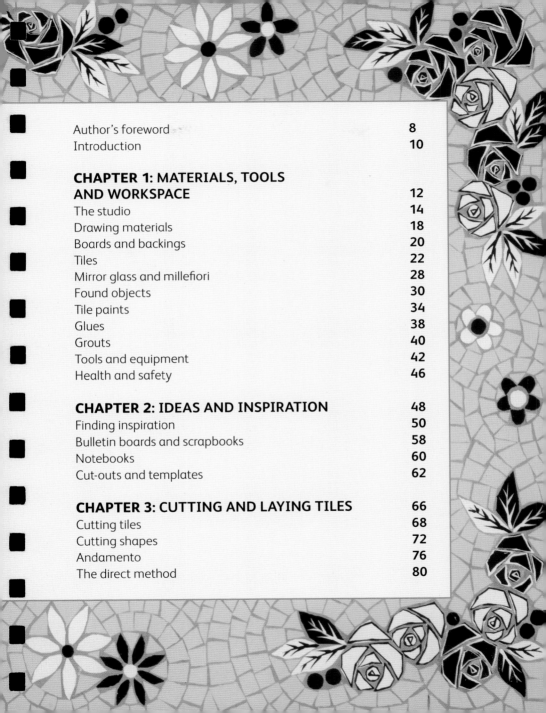

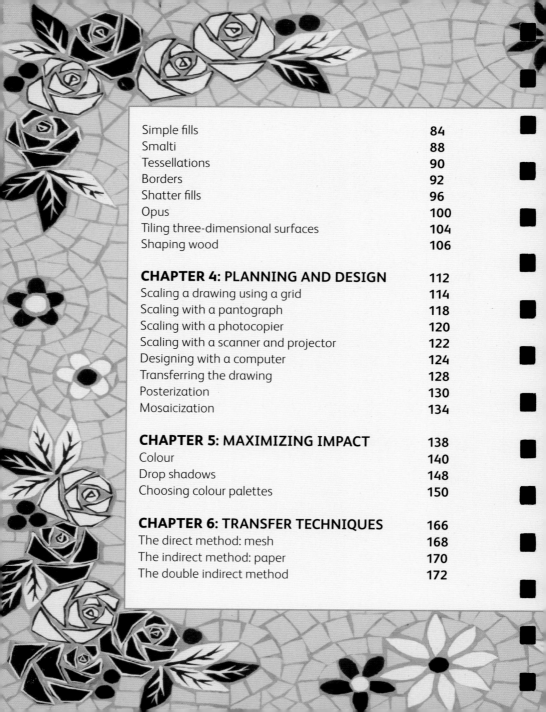

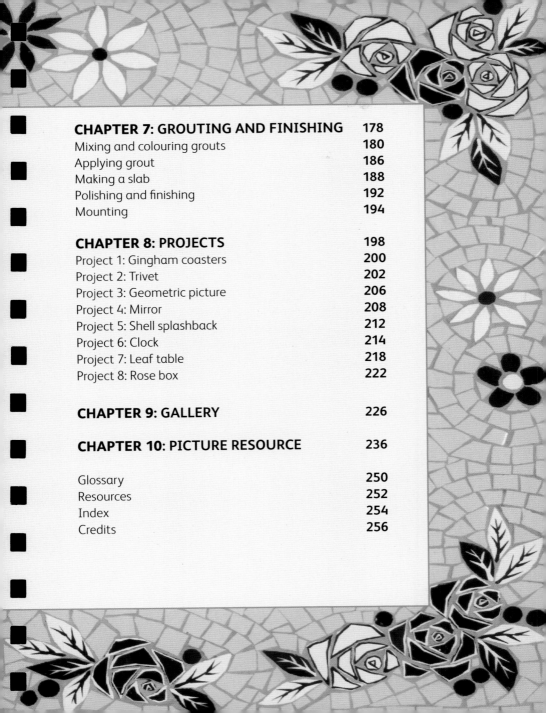

Author's foreword

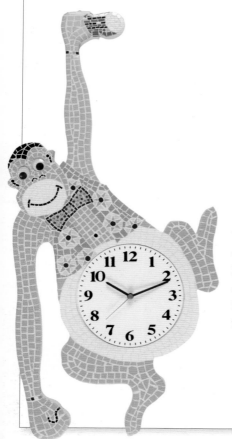

In this book I have tried to distil a lot of different areas of mosaic craft and put them down clearly and simply so they are practical and useful, as well as stimulating.

For me, "technique" is a broad term, and I would like this book to be more than just a manual about the mechanics of producing mosaics. As well as essential information on tools techniques and materials, there are also many suggestions for creative techniques: information on how to find ideas and hold on to them so that they are useful to you in the future; an exploration of colour and colour schemes; templates for mosaic motifs that you could use in your own pieces; a series of projects you could make at home; and a gallery of inspiring contemporary mosaics.

Whether you are just starting out with mosaics, or you are already an enthusiastic practitioner, I hope that the step-by-step guides, projects and creative ideas that are included here will inspire you, encouraging you to experiment and try new things.

TERESA MILLS

Introduction

RICH HISTORY
Below, top is a mosaic created by
the ancient Greeks, the inventors
of mosaics. Below, bottom is a
Moorish design. Both the Greeks
and the Moors contributed to the
rich history of mosaics.

Mosaics have a long history that stretches back several centuries BCE when the ancient Greeks first began to use coloured stones and pebbles to make geometric designs and then pictures. Over hundreds of years they developed these techniques into an art form that was also an industry, that used specially manufactured materials – the small tiles or "tesserae" made of stone or ceramics.

That skill and knowledge was passed seamlessly to the Romans, who further developed mosaics both as an art and a science, developing the manufacture and use of glass, and pushing further the decorative and pictorial effects that could be achieved. The Romans spread these techniques across the length and breadth of their empire.

There have been other great "flourishings" of mosaic art. During the Byzantine period in the eastern Mediterranean, churches were richly adorned with mosaics stretching from floor to ceiling. Byzantine mosaics can still be seen today – in Ravenna in Italy, for example. Later, Islamic artists of the Moorish empire took the art form in a different direction, producing exquisite patterns built on the perfection of mathematical ideas.

It is unlikely that the factors that produced these high points of the mosaic art form will ever again exist; these large, architectural

works were often the product of the efforts of hundreds of people, who, as well as being driven by shared beliefs, were also coerced by much harsher factors. It is worth remembering that many of those ancient mosaic "artists" would have been no more than slaves and treated just as brutally.

It is perhaps no wonder then that mosaics in the twenty-first century are very different. Mosaic artists today tend to work individually and on a much smaller scale. This does mean however that they are free to explore and play with ideas. There are so many directions in which you can take your own mosaic work: your designs can be strong and bold, or delicate and intricate; your colour choices can be bright and vibrant, or subtle and restrained. Yet the pleasure of making mosaics is little altered from when the technique was first developed.

ROMAN DEVELOPMENT
This Roman mosaic – situated in Istanbul – is more than 2,000 years old. The Romans took the skill of making mosaics from the Greeks and developed it further.

Materials, tools and workspace

Before you undertake any mosaic project you will need to obtain some basic materials and set up a suitable workspace. The following section introduces you to the tiles, adhesives, grouts and backing materials that you can choose from, and describes the tools that you will need to work with. However big or small the space available, the same rules apply to ensuring that your work area is well equipped, well lit, comfortable and safe.

The studio

Setting up a suitable workspace is important if you are going to enjoy your mosaicing — even if the only spare space you have is temporary use of a tabletop. Being comfortable as well as organized in whatever space is available will allow you to work productively and safely. This section introduces some of the important requirements for your "studio" — whether it is a dedicated room or a tray on your lap.

LIGHT

Probably the most important requirement for your workspace is good light — ideally, natural light from more than one window or skylight. Making mosaics requires a lot of closeup work and it is important that you can see what you are doing without straining your eyes. Natural light does not distort the colour of objects in the way that electric light does, but you will need a supplementary light-source to enable you to work at different times of day. A swing-arm lamp gives a good directional light that you can shine accurately onto your work; however, it is always good to work with more than one light-source to reduce shadows cast by your hands and tools as you work.

WORK SURFACE

It is easiest to work on mosaics at tabletop height. The work surface must be strong and stable. It will inevitably get marked and chipped, so don't use a valued piece of furniture. The work surface will also get wet if you use it for gluing and grouting. An old table or wooden worktop with a sealed or varnished surface is ideal. If you don't have space for an extra table and need to work on your kitchen or dining table, then buy an offcut of board or worktop that you can use as a work surface. (Always place a cloth or layers of newspaper between the surfaces to keep the good surface from being scratched.)

As well as being a practical space, your work area should also be somewhere where you can display objects and pictures that provide you with inspiration.

KEEP IT CLEAN

Try to "quarantine" your mosaic area from the rest of your living space – and sweep up regularly as you work. If you can, wear a dedicated pair of slippers or shoes in your mosaic area, and always wear an apron – this will reduce the amount of tile fragments that you carry into your living areas.

Keep an old household paintbrush to hand to clean the tile shards and offcuts from your piece as you work – never brush the piece clean with the back of your hand; the tile edges can cut you. Make your workspace a no-go area for pets and children – particularly when you are working!

You can greatly reduce the mess of mosaicing by having a large plastic container into which you cut your tiles – or you could even use a grocery bag. This will cut down the amount of waste that falls to the floor.

your hands and fingers. If you are susceptible to back pain, it may help to have a second work surface at a height that you can work at while standing to enable you to vary your position more frequently.

WET AREA

Not many homes offer the luxury of a spare sink in which to mix grouts and clean finished pieces. You will need to use a wash basin for cleaning and a bucket for mixing grouts. It makes sense, if the weather is reasonable, to do any cleaning and mixing outside whenever possible. If it's not possible outside, work on a plastic sheet well away from artwork, food and anything else you don't want contaminated with grout or dirty water.

Never dispose of old grout by washing it down a drain. If you mix grout in a plastic container, any excess can be left to dry completely then emptied into the bin – flexing the container and banging it against the inside of the dustbin will separate the grout from the walls of the container. Your sink of cleaning water should also be left to settle so that the grout residue sinks to the bottom – decant the water from the top and dispose of this down an outside drain. The remaining sludge should be emptied onto old newspapers that can then be folded and placed in the bin.

FLOORS

Avoid mosaicing on carpet if you can – a tiled or laminate floor is best so that you can easily sweep up tile fragments as you work. These fragments are sharp and will work their way into a carpet and damage it, or inflict a nasty cut on anyone walking across it with bare feet. If your workspace is carpeted throughout, buy a heavy-duty plastic worksheet and lay it down before starting a mosaic session.

A GOOD CHAIR

Find a comfortable chair – an office chair with an adjustable back and a variable, supportive seat is a good investment. If you spend long periods mosaicing it is very easy to settle in one position, and end up with back and muscle pain. Remember to pause and stretch regularly, and to rub and stretch

STORAGE

It is worth investing in a set of clear jars so you can see your tiles and find the right colours quickly. If you buy mixed batches of tiles, separate them into different containers before you start – that way you will not be hunting for an elusive matching tile with glue-covered hands. Separate storage areas for art materials, paints, glues and grouts – whether in the form of shelves or stackable boxes – will also make your life easier.

INSPIRATION

Try to preserve an area of wall or a bulletin board where you can collect and keep pictures and other scraps that stimulate ideas or suggest colour schemes.

Drawing materials

It is worth spending a little extra on good quality drawing materials, which produce the results you want and will last longer than cheaper alternatives. Store all your art materials in drawers or boxes so that you can find what you need when you need it.

◄ PENCILS

Graphite pencils are the basic drawing tools for developing your designs on paper and accurately drawing them up on the baseboard. A number and letter indicate the hardness or softness of a pencil. "Hard" pencils – H to 9H – are best for fine, accurate work. "Soft" pencils – B to 9B – leave a thicker, darker deposit and are useful for more freeform drawing, as well as for rubbing over the reverse of designs to transfer them.

▲ CHINAGRAPH PENCILS

Chinagraph, or grease, pencils are an alternate way to mark cutting guidelines on glass or ceramic tiles. These pencils have a core of solid, waxlike substance that will adhere to glossy surfaces.

▼ MARKERS

Permanent and semi-permanent markers are ideal for drawing onto glass and ceramic tiles to mark up difficult shapes. After cutting, residue can usually be removed with a soft cloth, aided by a solvent.

▲ WATER-BASED FIBRETIP PENS

Use water-based fibretip pens to colour in your drawings as you develop ideas and, once the design is transferred to the backing board or tiling surface, to show clearly where each colour is to be laid. For the latter purpose, buy cheap multipacks rather than expensive individual colours.

◄ PANTOGRAPH

A pantograph is a simple tool that provides an effective way to enlarge and reduce drawings. It is usually made from plastic or wood, and the arms and joints can be adjusted to produce copies of drawings to different scales. You can also find instructions on how to make your own on the internet.

▼ SET SQUARE

A set square is useful for marking up grids and checking that they are square.

▲ DRAFTSMAN'S TEMPLATES

Draftsman's templates are available from art suppliers and provide a quick way to draw perfect circles, ellipses and other simple shapes. They are ideal for marking up household tiles prior to cutting.

▼ LONG-ARMED COMPASSES

A long-armed pair of compasses is essential for creating perfect circles when drawing up larger designs such as clocks and tabletops. The arm is usually extendable and can accommodate a pencil or pen.

▼ LONG RULER/STRAIGHT EDGE

A long ruler or other straight edge is essential for drawing up grids for larger designs and mosaic murals.

partners
THE STATIONER

Boards and backings

The correct choice of board or backing for your mosaic depends on the conditions it is to be displayed in, for example, inside or outside, in the bathroom or a bedroom, and the tiles, adhesives, and laying technique you are using.

1 BACKER BOARD

Backer board is the best material to use for mosaics intended for a wet environment such as a bathroom. Backer board is sold under a variety of trade names; it is a lightweight, cement-based material that can be used to line existing floors and walls. The fixed board provides a robust tiling surface that will be unaffected even by soaking conditions.

Backer boards are available from building supply stores and specialist tile stores. Always follow the manufacturer's instructions carefully. Floors or walls may need a waterproof membrane between them and the backer board, with specified gaps to allow for expansion after installation. Cutting and jointing boards may also require the use of specialist tools and materials.

2 MDF (MEDIUM DENSITY FIBREBOARD)

MDF is an ideal baseboard material. It is relatively light and provides an even and stable surface to fix tiles to. MDF can be cut with standard tools and is widely available from DIY shops and building suppliers. Sheets normally go up 244 x 122 cm (8 x 4 ft) to and vary in thickness from 6 mm (¼ in) to 25 mm (1 in) – however, 12 mm (½ in) thick would be adequate for most of the projects in this book. Buying large sheets is generally most economical – some stores will cut the sheets for a small fee. If you are using this service, take along a cutting plan, or work out in advance a standard, simple subdivision of a whole board to give you baseboards that meet your needs.

The main shortcoming of MDF is that if it gets wet it will absorb water and swell – it is therefore not suitable for external locations or "wet" areas such as a bathroom. Before using MDF as a baseboard, it's important to prime it with PVA glue diluted with water.

MARINE PLY

3 Plywood consists of layers of wood bonded together, with the grain of each layer running in a different direction. This gives the bonded sheets great strength while remaining relatively lightweight. Marine ply, as its name suggests, is specifically manufactured for use in boat-building and is treated to prevent rotting. Marine ply can therefore be used as a baseboard for tiles in areas where there are high levels of moisture. However, it is important that all exposed surfaces of the board are thoroughly sealed using an external-grade varnish or paint to maximize the life of the material. Marine ply is available in a variety of thicknesses from 4 mm (⅜ in) up to 25 mm (1 in).

BROWN PAPER

4 Brown paper is used in the indirect method (see page 170) as a temporary support for tiles, which are glued to its surface using a water-soluble glue. Mosaic suppliers sell this paper in pre-cut sheets that are the right size to work on a design in sections. You can also buy brown paper in rolls for use in wrapping parcels – however, you should only use the uncoated type as it is essential that the paper can be thoroughly soaked to remove it after the tiles have been stuck in their permanent location.

MESH

5 Mosaic tile mesh is a flexible lightweight material – generally made from glass fibre – which allows you to assemble a mosaic on a workbench, then transfer it easily to where it is to be installed. Tiles are stuck to the mesh, normally with PVA glue. The sheets come in a variety of sizes, but generally it is sensible to work with pieces no more than 30 cm (1 ft) square, as bigger sheets are unmanageable when weighed down with tiles. Large designs can be created in sections and then assembled together on-site.

Tiles

There is an enormous range of tiles available to the mosaic artist
– specialist materials intended specifically for mosaics, as well as tiles
and materials primarily intended for home decoration. Each of these tile
types is described more fully in this section with a description of their
differing characteristics and how these affect both where you can use
them and how you can work with them. In the sections that follow there
are examples of other materials – natural materials and "found objects"
– which can also be used for mosaics or combined with tiles to extend
the range of options available.

Here, the same design has been
rendered using different tiles. On the
right, glass vitreous tiles are used
– including gold tiles, which add
richness and intricacy. On the left, a
combination of household ceramic
tiles and broken crockery is used.

*Quartered gold
tiles add lustre to
the finished piece.*

Square vitreous tiles are the mosaicist's "standard".

VITREOUS TILES

Composition: solid glass with colour uniformly distributed throughout the body of the tile.

Colour range: extensive range of pure colours and tints as well as exotic finishes such as pearlescent and metallic effects, and embedded gold leaf.

Dimensions: standard square, usually 20 mm (⅝ in).

Cost: varies according to colour and finish.

Application: the mosaicist's "standard" – ideal for both the direct and indirect methods (because the tile colour is clear even when working in reverse).

◆ A ridged or textured back facilitates adhesion.

◆ Bevelled edges hold grout.

◆ Readily available.

◆ Frost-proof, so suitable for outside use.

◆ Not recommended for floors because of brittleness and smoothness/slipperiness of surface.

◆ Can be spilt with circular-bladed cutters or "nibbled" with conventional tile nippers – beware of sharp edges and shards.

◆ Gold leaf backed tiles are hugely expensive, but provide effective "punctuation" within a piece. (These tiles are translucent glass backed with a thin foil in the same way as a mirror).

Vitreous tiles with gold and silver leaf backing.

Vitreous tiles with metallic streaks.

SMALTI

Composition: opaque coloured glass, square or rectangular in section, available in rods or as pre-cut tile-sized pieces.

Colour range: smalti are made exclusively for mosaic applications so a huge range of colours and finishes is available.

Dimensions: 8 mm (⅓ in) thick, 1.5 cm (⅔ in) long.

Cost: expensive – go for a "mixed bag" to begin with. You can always graduate to smalti containing 24-carat gold leaf later!

Applications: this is the classic mosaic material made from molten slabs of intensely coloured glass which is left to cool before being split and then further cut using a hammer and hardie (a chisel-like tool that is generally mounted in a wooden block, with which the smalti are cut).

◆ Ideal for picture making, but unsuitable for "practical" surfaces such as floors.

◆ Smalti are traditionally pressed into wet cement but left ungrouted as their surface contains small holes left by bubbles in the glass that would absorb grout.

Smalti are available in a stunning variety of colours.

HOUSEHOLD CERAMIC TILES

Composition: earthenware/clay tiles with a hard glazed surface.

Colour range: broad, but confined to a relatively subdued colour palette – pure primaries can be hard to come by.

Dimensions: various sizes from 5 to 30 cm (2 to 12 in); usually square though to rectangular, and sometimes octagon-shaped, tiles are also available. (Tiles of different sizes are often of different thickness so mix with care to avoid an uneven surface on the finished mosaic.)

Cost: generally cost-effective in terms of the area the tiles will cover – a drawback may be having to buy boxed or bulk quantities, so building up a broad palette of colours may require a large initial outlay. (If you can, find retailers who sell individual tiles.)

Applications: These are the wall tiles usually used in the home. The clay body of the tile is generally easy to cut; use a tabletop tile cutter to split them into smaller squares. The relative softness of the clay tile body makes them easy to shape with nippers. Using household tiles allows you to work with larger tile fragments.

◆ Generally these tiles are unsuitable for use on floors as they are too brittle and slippery.

◆ Not good for use with the indirect method as you cannot see the colour of the tile face (use the double indirect method instead, see page 172).

◆ These tiles are not weather resistant so avoid outdoor applications.

Household ceramic tiles come in many sizes and finishes.

PATTERNED CERAMIC TILES

Composition: as household ceramic tiles, but with a handpainted or transfer design under the glazed surface.

Colour range: a huge range of patterns is available, mostly in a repeat format to give a consistent effect when used in interior decorating.

Dimensions: most commonly in square format from 5 to 30 cm (2 to 12 in).

Cost: more costly than plain tiles – handpainted designs can be very expensive.

Applications: patterned tiles are more commonly used to provide detail and "points of interest" within a design. Often there may be a detail from within the tile that you want to utilize, which can mean discarding much of the body of the tile. These tiles are worked and shaped exactly like plain ceramic tiles; bear in mind the same points about suitability for different environments.

STONE

Composition: a range of different stones are quarried for architectural use and for flooring; these vary from soft limestone to hard granite and marble.

Colour range: stones offer a surprising range of colours from cool greens to bright reds and ochres.

Dimensions: from small mosaic-sized pieces up to very large slabs.

Cost: stone is expensive because of quarrying and transportation costs – generally it is only available from specialist suppliers, many of whom will not sell small amounts.

Applications: stone is difficult to work – generally a diamond-coated circular saw is required to cut it, which you would probably need to rent. Stone is great for outdoor applications, or indoors where its durability is important – worktops, fire-surrounds or floors for example. It is often easier to work on geometric designs that utilize pre-cut squares. Stone pebbles are also available; these tend to have a flat aspect and are uniformly sized, though randomly shaped, pieces of stone that allow you to produce crackle-effect areas.

TERRACOTTA TILES

Composition: plain clay tiles with a chunky, "rustic" look.

Colour range: natural clay colour, sometimes treated or crudely glazed – it is hard to obtain consistent colours across batches of tiles.

Dimensions: from small squares to slablike sizes – 5 to 46 cm (2 to 18 in).

Cost: handmade tiles can be expensive; the cost also depends on the size and finish.

Applications: these are hardwearing tiles, but always check the manufacturer's recommendations for use on floors and walls.

◆ Difficult to cut – the manufacturer will recommend suitable tools/machinery (which you may need to rent specially).

◆ Generally not suitable for detailed illustrative pieces. Often, small tiles are used uncut to create geometric patterns or textured effects.

◆ Unglazed tiles must be grouted with care and the surface treated with a sealant to prevent staining.

MARBLE

Composition: strictly, marble is a type of stone although it is often highly polished which gives it a very different, veined appearance.

Colour range: from white through to black, with reds and greens being the commonest colours.

Dimensions: available as rods, small tiles – about 25 mm (1 in) square, right up to large slabs for worktops and architectural applications.

Cost: can be hugely expensive, as marble is sourced from only a few geographical locations – most famously Carrera in Italy.

Applications: Marble rods are cut with a hammer and hardie to create smalti, which can be used to create mosaic pictures. For floors, worktops and large areas, pre-cut marble tiles are used in geometric designs.

Mirror glass and millefiori

Millefiori are little gems of coloured glass from Murano in Italy. Mirror glass is available in large sheets, which can be cut down to tile size pieces. Both can add eye-catching colour and interest to a mosaic.

Mirror glass is easily obtained but can be difficult to work with.

MIRROR GLASS

Colour range: most commonly, "silvered" mirror, although coloured mirror glass is available.

Composition: clear or tinted glass with a reflective metal foil coating on the "back" of the glass.

Dimensions: available in large sheets from glaziers to cut yourself or as small tile-sized pieces – 25 mm (1 in) square – often on a mesh backing.

Cost: offcuts from sheets of mirror glass from a glazier are the cheapest option although you will need to master cutting these to the size you require.

Applications: mirror glass has a very retro "glitterball" look so is not suitable for every situation! It is certainly not suitable for floors due to its brittleness and sharp edges.

◆ Use mirror glass within frames and borders.

◆ Always wear gloves and goggles when working with glass, it shatters unpredictably and the shards are particularly nasty.

◆ Cut mirror glass using a glazier's cutter – this is a penlike tool with a hardened wheel or diamond at the tip with which you score the surface of the glass and then snap over a raised edge.

MILLEFIORI

Composition: small circular or rectangular beads made from slices through rods of fused glass.

Colour range: each millefiori contains bright "blobs" of pure colours.

Dimensions: millefiori are typically 6–18 mm (¼–¾ inch) in diameter.

Cost: small quantities can be very expensive; look for specialist suppliers who may offer larger bags of mixed millefiori at more cost-effective prices.

Applications: millefiori – which comes from the Italian word meaning "thousand flowers" – suit tiny, intricate and rich designs. Use them in small pieces or as highlights or details within larger designs.

◆ Play around with the millefiori before gluing them down – it is important to select different diameters to pack them densely into an area, otherwise they will be swamped by grout.

◆ The different heights of millefiori can be a problem; you may need to pack shorter tiles with extra glue to get a uniform height.

◆ Millefiori look good embedded within a surface – if you have access to a router, try creating shapes or areas of a design in which to embed the millefiori (see page 106).

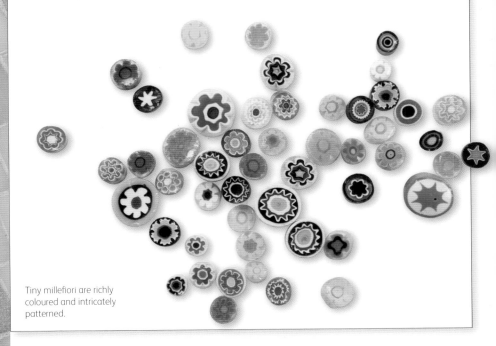

Tiny millefiori are richly coloured and intricately patterned.

Found objects

You are not confined to using manufactured glass or ceramic tiles in your mosaics. "Found" objects – recycled crockery and china as well as natural materials – provide a rich source of alternatives for creating complete mosaics, or as elements that you can combine with more conventional materials to give variation and interest to your designs.

BROKEN CHINA

Old cups and saucers or plates can provide a rich extra decorative element to your work. You can usually find suitable old china in charity shops or flea markets. This is also a wonderful way to recycle any accidentally broken treasured piece of china.

Break the crockery into smaller fragments by placing the pieces inside two plastic bags and hitting them with a hammer. Wearing gloves, sort through the pieces and clean up and shape the fragments with tile nippers if necessary. Watch out for shards of glaze left on the edges, as these can be razor sharp.

Flatter surfaces from plates are the easiest to work with – the curves of cups and bowls will make it more difficult to keep the surface of the mosaic flat, requiring you to break these items into smaller pieces.

Fragments of broken china provide another choice of material for the mosaicist.

Pebbles and stones are ideal for use in outdoor mosaics because they are unaffected by the weather.

PEBBLES

If you like beaches and the seashore, hunting for pebbles with which to create a mosaic design can be very satisfying. Look for rounded pebbles that are as flat as possible. Pick over a handful of stones at a time and select ones of similar sizes that contain interesting colours or veins. Sort them into groups, discarding any that vary too much in shape or are too big.

Many pebbles are porous so it is not wise to grout the mosaic because the pebbles will be stained by the grout. A better idea is to work straight into a thick layer of cement or combined tile grout/adhesive, pressing the pebbles in quite deeply. This technique effectively grouts the gaps between the pebbles from behind. It also allows you to make adjustments for the varying thickness of the pebbles by pressing the thicker ones in more deeply.

Pebbles are an excellent material for outdoor use – they are weatherproof as well as having good load-bearing properties. Pebble designs can add interest to patios and also work well as a decorative cover to ceramic planters.

LARGE STONES

Larger stones can make "super-sized" mosaics, although their weight means that their use is really confined to floor areas and slabs. Practically, it is better to source large stones from garden or building suppliers, who sell uniformly sized stones. Helping yourself to large quantities from a beach is frowned upon as well as illegal in many areas.

Working with large stones and pebbles is a skill that requires specific techniques, whether you are working directly on a design in situ, or using precast techniques to create slabs for later assemblage. It is essential that the design is built on strong foundations with sufficient concrete or hardcore underneath to prevent subsidence and cracking.

"BEACH-COMBED" GLASS

It will take you a long time to collect sufficient pieces of beach-combed glass to complete a mosaic. What you are looking for is fragments of old glass – usually bottles – that have been eroded and smoothed by long immersion in the sea. Hunting for these on a beach requires an eagle eye – most commonly you will find green pieces, with a frosted finish caused by the abrasion of the stones – but brown and white fragments are also there, although harder to find because of their similarity to the mass of pebbles.

Bottle fragments tend to be thin and relatively light and are therefore quite manageable to work with. Glue them to your baseboard with PVA or other clear-drying adhesive, as the glue will be partially visible through the glass.

Some beach combed glass including "rare" red and blue fragments.

SHELLS

Shells can provide an interesting decorative effect when used as the tiles within a mosaic. You can collect suitably sized small shells yourself – again, give consideration to the environmental impact of this – or you can buy them from specialist shops.

Most shells, particularly the smaller ones that you are most likely to use, are very delicate, so their applications are limited. You can partially reinforce shells by packing them with the cement or adhesive you are using before placing them in the mosaic. The porosity of shells means that you can't grout them so, as with pebbles, work with a thick layer of cement or dual-purpose grout/adhesive, pressing them in well so they "self grout". When the mosaic is complete you can paint the shells with a layer of clear polyurethane varnish, which will help protect them, as well as enhancing their colour with a "wet-look" effect.

DIAMANTÉ AND RHINESTONES

These "simulated diamonds" are widely available from craft suppliers. While they are not really suitable as a mosaic material, they can be added to the surface of a finished mosaic to act as a decorative detail or "highlight". Use a suitable clear-drying adhesive – "superglue" is ideal – using just a tiny spot for each single piece. Additions like these are not hardwearing, so confine their use to pictorial rather than functional pieces.

BUTTONS

You can buy huge bags of buttons from haberdashery shops for a very small cost. These can be glued onto a finished piece, or if you have a sufficient quantity, play around with mosaic designs using groups of buttons as your tiles. A thin MDF or thick card will make an adequate baseboard. Use a general-purpose adhesive sparingly, having first played around with the buttons to pack them as tightly together as possible. Leave the finished piece ungrouted, perhaps mounting it when dry behind glass in a frame.

GLASS SHAPES

You can now obtain a huge variety of glass shapes – animals, butterflies, hearts, geometric shapes, flowers and so on – moulded in glass, both plain and coloured. These provide another way of adding a bit of fun and interest to some mosaic subjects. Again, use a specialist glass adhesive or "superglue" to fix them firmly to the surface of your finished mosaic.

GLASS GEMS

Another material widely available from art and craft stores, glass gems are uniformly sized and come in different coloured tints. Although not really suitable for using as substitute tiles, they can provide attractive "punctuation marks" on the surface of your design, and work particularly well as adornments to water-themed pieces.

Tile paints

Hand painting household tiles with specialist tile paints allows you to embellish your mosaics. You can use tile paints to add detail and decorative patterns, or to create "solid" colours that would otherwise be difficult to come by. Unlike glazes, tile paints do not require a kiln to heat them to a very high temperature – they are designed to be fired in a domestic oven. However, the lower temperature firing means that the finished surface is not as durable as a true glaze – you should therefore avoid using them in areas where the tiles will be subject to wear or abrasion. Painted tile fragments work well on pictures and frames that are designed to be hung up and therefore receive minimal wear and tear.

Tools

Cleaning cloth
Paintbrushes
Domestic oven
Baking tray or aluminium foil

Materials

Ceramic tiles
Tile paints

DIFFERENT APPROACHES

You could cut different shapes from ceramic tiles – flowers or leaves for example – and then paint them, or alternatively, decorate whole ceramic tiles with abstract patterns.

1 Clean the tiles

Make sure that the tiles you are going to paint on are thoroughly clean and dry and free from any surface dust or grease. Grease in particular will stop the paint from keying evenly to the surface of the tiles

2 Apply details

Detail is applied to tiles with a fine brush – it is worth investing in good quality brushes that hold the paint well and leave an even, flowing stroke. You need to work freehand – ink or chinagraph lines would discolour the paints – so practise on scraps of unwanted tiles first. Work through the areas of the design in a logical order so that you don't smudge the areas you have completed. Here, the flower centres and petals were painted first.

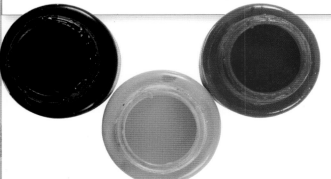

Ceramic paints are available in a broad spectrum of colours.

3 Develop the design

Next add the leaves and polka dots. Polka dots are a simple way to add interest to plain areas of a design. Allow the paints to dry thoroughly before moving onto the next step to avoid the colours running into each other.

4 Paint the outlines

Dark outlines give the flowers and leaves form – use a very fine brush and try to make each line with a single stroke. Concentrate on the movement of your hand – repeat the same tick-like gesture to produce each line, rather than drawing the shape carefully, which generally leads to a "shaky" result.

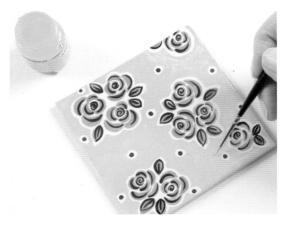

5 Fill in the background

In this example, the yellow background is painted around the design to give the interest of the tile colour showing through around the edges of the painted area. (If you want a completely flat background to the tile, paint this onto the tile first using a wide brush, and allow it to dry thoroughly before starting to paint the design itself.)

6 "Fire" the tiles

Leave the finished design to dry thoroughly, then place the tiles on an old baking tray or a sheet of aluminium foil and bake in the oven at the specified temperature – as with everything, follow the manufacturer's instructions carefully. Don't be tempted to over-fire the tiles as some colours will lose their lustre if they are baked for too long.

7 Split the tiles

Slice each tile into strips using a tabletop tile cutter, and then split each of these strips into small, square tiles. Keep any leftover painted fragments; you never know when you might find a use for them as a "found object" in another design or picture.

Glues

You will need a number of different glues when producing mosaics. Which glue you use depends on the tiles you are using, the type of backing and the environment in which the mosaic is to be housed.

PVA GLUE

PVA glue is white in the bottle but transparent/translucent when dry. It is the ideal glue for mounting tiles to most surfaces, particularly MDF and other wood-based boards. Make sure you select a waterproof type – the glues used by carpenters in exterior woodwork are perhaps the most reliable.

Waterproof PVA glues are commonly used to mount tiles on wooden backing boards.

WASHABLE CRAFT GLUE

Washable craft glue is similar to PVA, but you can loosen this glue by dampening it, making it ideal when you are using brown paper or some other material as a temporary support when "working in reverse" (see the indirect method, page 170). You may find you need to dilute the glue further with a little water so that the mix is slightly weaker and easier to soak off at a later stage.

CLEANING BRUSHES

After using PVA based glues you need to wash brushes thoroughly in warm soapy water. Dried PVA is resistant to almost any attempt to remove it and you will have no choice but to discard your brushes if you do not clean them immediately after use.

EPOXY RESIN

Epoxy resin is a two-component adhesive that will bond permanently to almost any surface – ideal for quick fixes and repairs, particularly for outside applications. Squeeze each component from its container so that equal amounts are side by side on an old tile or plate. Mix them thoroughly with a stick and use the mixture fairly quickly. The setting time varies, but normally you should make no more than you can comfortably use in twenty minutes.

This type of dispenser makes it easier to mix the correct quantities of two-component epoxy glues.

MASKING TAPE/PACKING TAPE

Masking tape and packing tape are useful as temporary support to hold tiles in place while a glue sets – particularly when you are working vertically, for example when installing a mosaic and adding tiles to cover screws and other fittings.

SAND AND CEMENT

Sand and cement are used for floors and exterior applications – the same mix is used as both an adhesive and as the grout between the mosaic pieces. Usually three parts of sand to one part cement are mixed dry, then water is added a little at a time until a workable but thick consistency is achieved. "Sharp" sand of the type used to render walls is best to use. You can buy small bags of "ready mix", intended for small repairs to paths and walls This is useful if you have nowhere to store the large, standard sacks of separate sand and cement that are generally supplied to builders.

A wide packing tape on the left, a narrower masking tape on the right.

Grouts

There are a variety of grouts available with which to finish your mosaic piece. Budget and the storage space you have available will determine your choice as much as the tiles you are using.

Ready-mixed grouts should be transferred from larger to smaller containers when in use, to prevent your stock from drying out.

READY-MIXED GROUT

Ready-mixed grout is the simplest and most readily available form of grout, and is sold premixed in resealable tubs. Ready-mixed grout is intended for use with domestic wall tiles and can be applied straight from the container without you having to adjust the consistency. For most mosaic projects this type of grout is ideal, providing the finished piece is sited indoors. Ready-mixed water-resistant grouts are also made specifically for use in bathrooms — however, it is not generally advisable to use these grouts in an exterior location.

Ready-mixed grouts are usually white, although you may also come across a limited range of colours. For most projects you will want to tone down the grout to keep it from breaking up the design — see the section on colouring grout to understand how to go about this (page 180).

CEMENT-BASED GROUTS

Cement-based grouts are sold as a dry powder that you mix with water. While these grouts do work out somewhat cheaper than the ready-mixed variety, this benefit is often outweighed by the need for careful mixing and the fact that any excess has to be discarded rather than saved and reused. However, some mosaicists prefer this type of grout, claiming that it fills the gaps between tiles more completely and with less shrinkage. Certainly you should experiment with these grouts at some stage – but follow the instructions carefully, and wear a mask and gloves when you are mixing. Cement grouts are most commonly grey or white in colour, although a very limited choice of other colours may be available.

EXTERIOR GROUTS

Exterior grouts are cement-based grouts with additives that make them more resistant to moisture and extremes of temperature.

Foil baking containers are strong enough to mix cement-based grouts in, and can be discarded after use.

EPOXY GROUT

Epoxy grout is a two-component grout intended to provide a seal to tiles that is not only completely waterproof, but also resistant to corrosive substances. This grout is particularly suitable for kitchen worktops and other areas that will be subjected to a range of temperatures and will need to withstand the use of strong cleaning materials. Epoxy grouts can be difficult to apply – once mixed they "cure" rapidly, so only mix a small amount at a time. You will find you need stiff squeegees and tools to work the grout into your tiles as it has a thicker consistency than ordinary grout. Epoxy grout is also quite costly.

Tools and equipment

You need a few basic tools to create mosaics — buy the best you can
afford and clean them after each session to remove glue and tile waste.
Looked after in this way, tile cutters and other tools will last a lifetime.

TILE CUTTING TOOLS

▲ NIPPERS
Nippers are used for cutting and
shaping glass tesserae and household
tiles. The spring ensures you can
work one-handed while you hold
the tile in your other hand. Invest in
good-quality nippers with tempered,
well-aligned jaws.

▲ WHEELED CUTTERS
Wheeled cutters (such as
"Leponitt") have circular
carbide cutting disks that
can be rotated as the edges
wear. They are very useful
for splitting vitreous tiles
consistently into halves
and quarters.

▶ TABLETOP TILE CUTTER
Tabletop tile cutters are used by
professional household tilers, but
you can also use these "scribe
then crack" cutters to quickly
split larger household tiles into
strips that you can then break
with nippers into evenly-sized
mosaic squares.

GLUING AND GROUTING TOOLS

▼CONTAINERS
Containers of different sizes
can hold glue and sorted tiles
as you work.

▲FOIL CONTAINERS
Foil containers and trays intended for storing
food are sealable and will extend the life of
mixed grouts and glues.

◄SPONGES
Sponges are essential for cleaning down the mosaic after
grouting – buy them cheaply and in bulk from grocery
stores, as the tile edges will quickly destroy them.

▸SQUEEGEES
A variety of plastic or rubber-bladed squeegees are
available for grouting. The squeegee simultaneously
presses grout into the gaps between tiles while
clearing the tile surface of excess grout.

▲TOOTHPICKS AND TWEEZERS
For really detailed work you will find fingers alone
too clumsy to position the tiniest pieces of mosaic
accurately. Position small tiles with tweezers and use
a toothpick to align the tesserae.

▲COTTON BUDS
Cotton buds are ideal for cleaning up small areas
of finished mosaics. Use them to remove excess
glue and grout and to polish areas of detail.

TOOLS FOR MAKING AND MOUNTING BASEBOARDS

▾ SAW
A long household saw is the best tool with which to accurately cut large square or rectangular baseboards – the saw is "self-guiding" and will produce a straight cut much more easily than smaller hand saws.

▴ SANDING BLOCK
A sanding block is useful for cleaning up baseboards after sawing, to remove any rough edges.

▾ JIGSAW
A jigsaw is an electric hand saw with a narrow blade that allows you to cut backing boards into a variety of shapes.

▴ ROUTER
A router is an electric-powered woodworking tool used to hollow out shapes from the surface of a board so that tiles can be set flush with the surface.

▲ CORK STICKERS AND FELT
Use cork stickers and felt to back objects such
as coasters and trivets to prevent damage to
tabletops and work surfaces in your home.

OTHER USEFUL EQUIPMENT

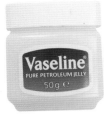

▲ PETROLEUM JELLY
Petroleum jelly is used as a release
agent when tiling slabs within a
frame – it stops cement or grout
adhering to the interior of the
frame and makes removal of the
finished slab easier.

▲ CLINGWRAP
Clingwrap provides an extra seal around
containers to increase the shelf life of
mixed paints, grouts and glues.

▶ CLEAN-UP BRUSH
A household paintbrush is useful for
cleaning your piece as you go along, to
clear away both dust and sharp splinters.

Health and safety

When working in any craft medium, it is important to treat the materials you use with respect, to understand their properties, and to be sensible in how you work with them. Making mosaics does sometimes require using fairly unpleasant materials such as specialist glues and grouts. Always make sure you read the manufacturer's information about any product you are using, and follow all the recommendations to do with health and safety. At the very least make sure you have the items listed on these pages available. You will find you create far fewer problems for yourself if you clean up as you go along, sweeping up tile waste and keeping your workspace clear and organized.

GLOVES

Workman's gloves, made from leather or padded cotton, are a sensible precaution, particularly when cutting household glass or mirror glass. Strong rubber gloves are essential when you apply grout. Latex gloves – the type worn by doctors – are useful when performing detailed work such as painting or cleaning up finished mosaics.

GOGGLES

Working on mosaics means cutting and shaping glass and ceramics with a variety of tools. Inevitably, tiles will sometimes shatter and break unpredictably causing shards and splinters to fly off in all directions. The most important thing when cutting your tiles is to protect your eyes by wearing appropriate goggles or lighter-weight safety glasses. If you do get tile dust or fragments in your eye, rinse thoroughly using an eye bath. Never try to remove foreign matter with your fingers or by rubbing your eyes – the splinters can be very sharp and you risk permanently damaging your eyes. If particles do not wash out, then seek medical help.

DUST MASKS

When cutting or drilling tiles or baseboards – particularly if you are using power tools such as jigsaws or circular saws, make sure you wear an approved safety mask to prevent dust from getting into your lungs. Masks that can be shaped to cover both your mouth and nose are best – simple paper "cone" masks that sit on your face offer little benefit. Remember that any dust mask is not intended to filter out solvent fumes from paints or adhesives. It is best to avoid any materials that require you to wear a specialist safety mask and chemical filters – for most applications, whether gluing, grouting, sealing or painting, you should be able to find a safer and easier alternative.

VENTILATED AREA

When you are working in a way that produces dust or requires the use of chemicals, it is essential that you work in a well-ventilated environment. In most cases, unless you have a workspace with specialist ventilation, this will mean working out of doors, and if need be waiting for good weather to allow you to begin or complete specific tasks such as cutting boards or mixing cement-based grouts.

2

Ideas and inspiration

You can find ideas for exciting and original mosaic designs from many sources. This chapter is about training your eyes to spot the things that will inspire you. Equally importantly, it suggests ways of organizing these sources of inspiration so that you can create a useful resource of ideas that you will refer to again and again.

Finding inspiration

You can find ideas to develop your own mosaic work from many sources: a piece of fabric, a vintage children's book or maybe a delicate leaf. The world around you is full of natural and manmade objects that can inspire design ideas. Keep your eyes open for inspiration whether you're visiting an art gallery, walking on the beach or looking through an old box of greeting cards. Find a place to store and record the many different things you come across.

CHILDREN'S DRAWINGS

Children's pictures are often inspiring due to their simplicity, and the unselfconscious way in which children put colours together and reduce things to simple shapes. You could, for example, mosaic a tabletop based on your children's drawings, traced and enlarged (perhaps with their signatures, too). Such objects are a beautiful way to preserve memories of the fleeting years of childhood.

Base designs on children's drawings.

BOOK AND COMIC ILLUSTRATIONS

Old book illustrations – particularly books that pre-date full-colour and photographic printing – often use a limited number of colours in flat areas that can be adapted to make a mosaic design. Comic strips are often even "purer" drawings, with the elements simplified into simple lines and two or three colours that can be enlarged into dramatic motifs.

Vintage children's books provide a wealth of colourful ideas.

PAPER AND PACKAGING

Wrapping paper is a rich source of abstract designs. You can easily keep remnants of paper in a scrapbook or file and refer to them when you are looking for patterns and backgrounds to use in your own designs.

Packaging materials and labels often contain colourful and bold motifs that are suitable for enlarging to use within a mosaic design. Wrapping paper offers strong two-dimensional motifs that you can easily cut out or copy using a lightbox.

FABRIC

Any number of exciting design ideas can come from the different fabrics around your home. Curtains, upholstery, cushions, rugs, all styles of clothes – even a dishtowel – may all contain a huge variety of different colour combinations, patterns and pictorial elements. You can collect swatches of material to refer to when looking for suitable colours to use in a design, and extend your collection by looking in charity shops, or visiting online auction sites where you can find a truly amazing variety of fabrics from around the world.

Knitted patterns and crocheted materials are often particularly suitable for adaptation into mosaic designs; they adhere to a simple geometric grid in the same way that mosaic patterns usually do. However, patchwork quilting is probably the fabric variant that most closely resembles mosaics. Each piece of the patchwork is, effectively, a cloth "tile" – some quilts you could almost duplicate using patterned pieces of tiles cut to the same shape and size.

▲ Crocheted patchwork and knitwear – such as this Fair Isle sweater – are ideal sources of inspiration for the mosaicist.

◀ ▼ Vintage textiles contain many motifs and colour combinations that can be turned into a mosaic design.

◄ Items from the home – like these cushions – can provide a source of ideas as well as help you create mosaics that "fit" with their surroundings.

▲ A selection of strongly abstract, vintage fabric designs.

◄ Even dishtowels can offer strong design ideas – the floral motif on the right suggested the colour scheme for the Trivet project (see page 202).

CHINA

Household crockery and floor and wall tiles are other readily available references for the mosaic artist. You can collect old pottery and tiles quite inexpensively – their condition is not too important as the odd chip or crack won't affect their value to you. Storage is a potential problem with three-dimensional objects, but if you can find a storage area – perhaps on a shelf at the back of a cupboard – you will find the repertoire of design ideas they contain very useful. Some hand-painted crockery contains designs and motifs that you can almost copy directly – for example, pottery from the 1950s and 1960s often has a strong calligraphic quality. (Don't worry too much about copying ideas for your own use – but copying designs for pieces that you are going to sell could be a breach of copyright.)

▲ A mixed collection of 1950s-style and contemporary black and white crockery provides inspiration for painting your own tiles and a reference for interesting abstract shapes.

◀ Stripes and polka dots are elements that the mosaicist can easily adapt and reproduce in their own designs.

▶ These hand-painted Italian ceramics have inspired many of the colour schemes of pieces in this book. the leaf table project (see page 218) uses a colour palette that draws heavily from this collection of tableware.

OTHER OBJECTS

If you look around your home you will see shapes, lines, colours and patterns everywhere that could be used in a design for a mosaic. As well as looking around, gather together a broad collection of items from shells and other natural objects to tins, glassware and children's toys.

▲Tins, whether vintage or new, provide a source of pictorial ideas and suggestions for colour combinations – with the practical advantage that they can also be used to store materials.

▼These old pieces of hand-painted glassware show how a few simple brushstrokes can create realistic and enchanting pictorial elements – techniques that you can learn from when painting your own tiles.

▲Shells and other objects found in nature can be a great source of inspiration, as well as a material for creating mosaics.

◀ Enamelware and 1970s crockery share a similar use of strong motifs and an almost overwhelming choice of colour. Designs like this translate very easily into mosaic motifs.

▼ A collection of quirky objects that are interesting for their shape and colour – the jar lid is the basis of the design used in the gingham coasters project (see page 200).

◀ Children's toys are a source of simple and "characterful" shapes.

Bulletin boards and scrapbooks

A bulletin board above your work area – or a scrapbook close at hand – are excellent ways of recording ideas and inspiration. Get into the habit of collecting and keeping things that you find visually interesting or unusual – whether it is a torn-off corner of wrapping paper, a photograph you have taken or a postcard of a painting that you particularly like. Add a brief note as to why you found an item interesting and what you think its application might be.

What is often interesting about the things you collect in this way is the juxtaposition between them – try to keep things flexible and move things around to play with ideas. If you have the space, a bulletin board is especially useful in this respect, as it allows you to change things around and provides a constant reminder of the inspirational things that you have come across.

SCRAP BOX

It may be that what interests you won't fit into a two-dimensional book – pieces of china or natural objects like shells and pebbles, for example. In this case, create a "scrap box" – perhaps using an old shoebox – so that you can keep any three-dimensional objects that take your fancy. Try to add items to your scrap box regularly, and search through them frequently to remind yourself of beautiful things or clever ideas that you might be able to turn into a mosaic design.

This scrap box contains all sorts of images and things collected when travelling: postcards from art exhibitions and of the Byzantine mosaics in Ravenna, Italy, as well as illustrations clipped from magazines and catalogues.

BULLETIN BOARD

A bulletin board ensures that inspirational sources are always in view. Some of the things on this board are:

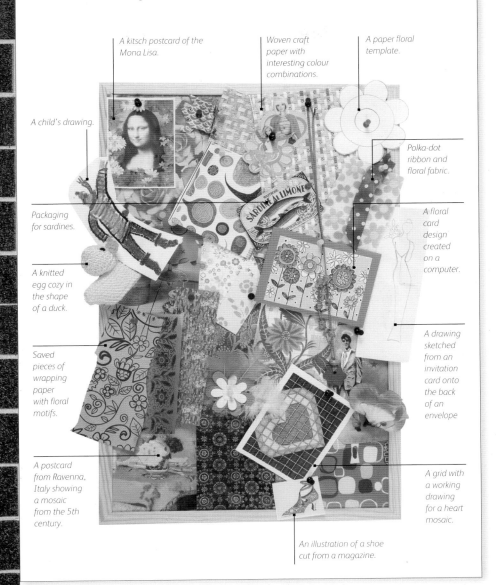

A kitsch postcard of the Mona Lisa.

Woven craft paper with interesting colour combinations.

A paper floral template.

A child's drawing.

Polka-dot ribbon and floral fabric.

Packaging for sardines.

A floral card design created on a computer.

A knitted egg cozy in the shape of a duck.

Saved pieces of wrapping paper with floral motifs.

A drawing sketched from an invitation card onto the back of an envelope

A postcard from Ravenna, Italy showing a mosaic from the 5th century.

A grid with a working drawing for a heart mosaic.

An illustration of a shoe cut from a magazine.

Notebooks

It is a good idea to use a simple notebook to keep a log of each project as you proceed with it. You don't have to be too detailed, but it is good to record things that go right (and those that don't) for future reference. Keeping this information in one place means that you can easily refresh your memory about a particular technique or material when you want to try something similar in the future.

RECORDING YOUR WORK

For example, use your log to record how to make up different adhesives, or the different materials you needed to complete a certain area. You can think of the log as your "mosaic recipe book" which will help you to quickly repeat successful techniques and avoid repeating past failures. In addition, a digital camera means that you can record your work and keep a visual log on your computer or print out the pictures to add into your notebooks.

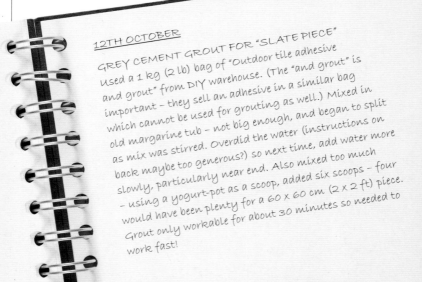

12TH OCTOBER

GREY CEMENT GROUT FOR "SLATE PIECE"
Used a 1 kg (2 lb) bag of "Outdoor tile adhesive and grout" from DIY warehouse. (The "and grout" is important – they sell an adhesive in a similar bag which cannot be used for grouting as well.) Mixed in old margarine tub – not big enough, and began to split as mix was stirred. Overdid the water (instructions on back maybe too generous?) so next time, add water more slowly, particularly near end. Also mixed too much – using a yogurt-pot as a scoop, added six scoops – four would have been plenty for a 60 x 60 cm (2 x 2 ft) piece. Grout only workable for about 30 minutes so needed to work fast!

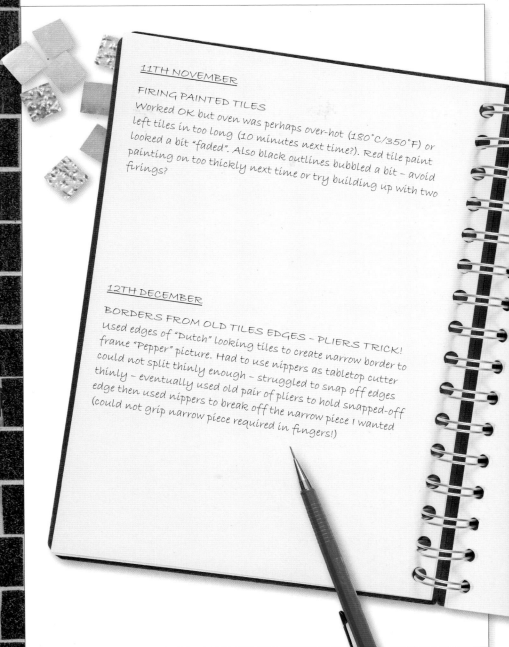

11TH NOVEMBER

FIRING PAINTED TILES

Worked OK but oven was perhaps over-hot (180°C/350°F) or left tiles in too long (10 minutes next time?). Red tile paint looked a bit "faded". Also black outlines bubbled a bit – avoid painting on too thickly next time or try building up with two firings?

12TH DECEMBER

BORDERS FROM OLD TILES EDGES – PLIERS TRICK!

Used edges of "Dutch" looking tiles to create narrow border to frame "Pepper" picture. Had to use nippers as tabletop cutter could not split thinly enough – struggled to snap off edges thinly – eventually used old pair of pliers to hold snapped-off edge then used nippers to break off the narrow piece I wanted (could not grip narrow piece required in fingers!)

Cut-outs and templates

A very simple technique to help you build and develop your mosaic designs is to use paper cut-outs. Cut-outs can help you to produce strong, striking designs by overlaying and repeating simple shapes. This is a particularly useful technique if you feel your own drawing skills are limited. You can use paper cut-outs just as a design tool, or as full-sized templates to work with directly onto the mosaic baseboard.

Tools
Pencil
Circle template
Scissors

Materials
Paper
Tracing paper
MDF or similar
Masking tape

DESIGNING WITH CUT-OUTS

Cut-outs can be used to develop the composition of your design, allowing you to move around and experiment with different elements. Using cut-outs saves you from repeatedly redrawing a design and enables you to develop ideas quite quickly.

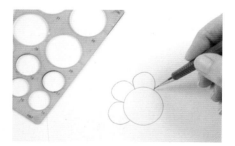

1 Draw simple shapes
You can use any cheap paper to draw your templates on. For this vase design, simple flower and petal shapes were first drawn by hand. Or, trace or cut-out elements from other sources – perhaps from wallpaper, or illustrations in magazines. When using cut-outs as a design tool, you don't need to work full-size – you can always scale up the finished design later.

2 Cut out the shapes
Using scissors to carefully cut around the shapes. At this stage you could also colour in the cut-outs with markers, although you may find introducing colour a distraction best left until the structure and shape of the design is decided. Build up a stock of cut-outs – you may want to copy some of the shapes so you have "repeats" of these elements.

3 Position design "anchors"

Tape down a sheet of paper as your background – cutting it to your preferred size and shape first – then start to position the main elements of the design. In this case, the large circular shape of the vase is a key element to establish first. Try positioning main elements off-center, or even running off the "frame", to introduce variation. Then start positioning other main elements within the frame – in this case, the larger flower heads.

4 Build up the design

Add other elements, but keep everything flexible – keep pushing elements around. The beauty of using cut-outs is that you can easily move and overlay different elements – try the same elements in a different "order" in the picture, perhaps bringing a background element to the front, or masking other elements to create new shapes and combinations. You can quickly add or modify things if you feel something is missing – such as here, adding some sharper petal shapes or two or three larger flower heads.

5 Trace the finished design

When you are completely happy with the look of the design, carefully lay a larger piece of tracing paper over the picture and tape this down. Then, using a pencil, carefully trace around the design to produce the final drawing. You can then transfer this to the baseboard (see page 128).

USING CUT-OUTS AS MOSAIC TEMPLATES

You can also use cut-outs as full-size templates. This is an ideal way to work with a repeat pattern – a design in which an identical element is repeated a number of times. Using cut-outs is much easier than tracing and transferring a drawing; repeated elements need only be drawn once and this ensures that each repeat is nearly identical.

1 **Draw up the design**
Begin by drawing your design onto a piece of paper – in this case, a simple Paisley motif. The drawing should be the same size as you want the element to be in the finished mosaic.

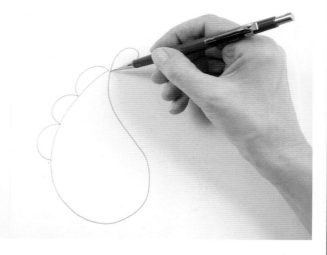

2 **Make a cut-out**
Cut carefully around your design to make a cut-out – you can then simply draw around this on other sheets of paper to make more cut-outs of the same motif if you wish.

3 Position the cut-outs

Work with the paper cut-outs directly on your prepared baseboard. You can see instantly the effect of spacing and positioning the cut-outs differently. Try adding cut-outs to see how crowded you can make the design, then try simplifying and refining the piece by taking elements away. In this example, some of the cut-outs have been "flipped".

4 Draw around the templates

Once you are happy with the look of your design, draw around the cut-outs onto the baseboard. (To keep things from moving around, hold the cut-outs in place temporarily using pieces of masking tape.)

5 Cut the template more

If your shape contains more details, then you can cut down one of your original templates to produce another template. Use this to help you copy the detail within each of the outline shapes produced from the first template.

3 Cutting and laying tiles

The basis for all mosaic making is being able to accurately and consistently cut tiles to perfectly fit your design, and then to lay and glue them neatly and evenly. These are skills that are only developed through practice. However, with persistence, you will develop these abilities to the point where you will amaze yourself. This chapter takes you from the basics of cutting simple shapes, through to the complex fills that more advanced projects might require.

Cutting tiles

Learning to cut tiles accurately is the basic skill that every mosaicist needs – it takes time and patience to acquire the knack of accurately splitting tiles. But once you have mastered the techniques and can consistently produce tile pieces to the shape and size you need, you will find that your mosaic work really takes off – allowing you to work quickly and creatively. As with any skill, practice and more practice is the key to success.

Tools

Nippers

Tabletop tile cutter

Materials

Vitreous tiles

Household ceramic tiles

Glass tesserae

GLASS TILES

Vitreous (glass) tiles are hard but brittle, and are likely to shatter unpredictably when you first begin to work with them. From the beginning it is important to take care and to follow simple safety procedures to avoid cutting yourself on the waste that cutting produces. Use appropriate safety wear (particularly eye protection) and keep your work area as free as possible from a build-up of sharp debris and shards.

Nippers

1 Practise using the tile nippers
The mosaicist's main tool is a pair of tile nippers – it is worth investing in a really good pair with hardened and well-aligned cutting edges. Take the nippers in your right hand if you are right-handed, or your left if left-handed, and hold the tile between the thumb and forefinger of your other hand.

2 Cut a little way into the tile
Squeeze the nipper handles just enough to hold the tile in the jaws of the nipper, then check and adjust the alignment of the tile. Don't put too much of the tile into the jaws – about one-third of the width of a standard sized tile at most. If you attempt to cut more, the resistance of the tile will be too much, forcing you to "grab" at the tile handles, which will just cause the tile to shatter.

3 Apply gradual pressure
Gradually increase the pressure of your grip on the handles of the nippers, gripping the tile more firmly between the thumb and index finger of your other hand and twisting the nippers slightly. The idea is to create a fault-line that the tile splits along – a line that is a continuation of the nipper blades. In reality, the first few times you try this, the tile will likely split in completely the wrong way and be reduced to powder and splinters. Keep trying – with practice and patience you will begin to get the results you want.

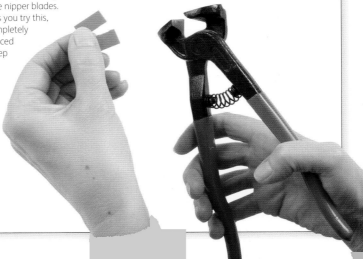

HOUSEHOLD TILES

Ceramic household tiles are easier to cut than glass tiles – the glazed surface of these tiles is very thin, while the clay base of the tile is relatively soft and crumbly. However, you also need to approach cutting these tiles with care – sometimes an exposed glazed surface can be razor-sharp and inflict a nasty wound if you are careless when handling the tiles.

1 Using a tabletop tile cutter
A tabletop tile cutter, obtainable quite cheaply from most DIY stores, can be used to split household tiles into strips. The cutter normally has a moveable arm or wheel with a cutting blade that scores the surface of the tile. Cutters like these are made in large sizes capable of cutting thick floor tiles.

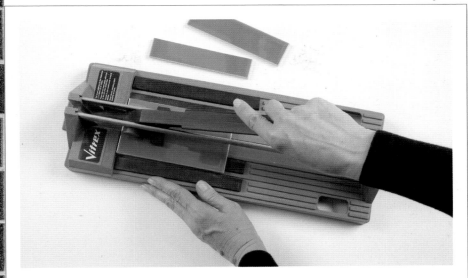

2 Cut the tiles into strips

Place a tile into the cutter about 6 to 12 mm (¼ to ½ in), then move the arm along to score the surface of the tile. Once the tile is scored, bear down on the lever of the cutter to snap the tile along the scored line. This should produce a neat strip of tile. You will need to practise a few times to understand how much pressure is needed to cut into the surface of the tile, and how much to bear down on the lever to get the tile to break. Work across the tile, breaking it into equal-size strips.

3 Make mosaic pieces

Once you have produced several tile strips using the cutter, use the tile nippers to snap each strip into pieces. You can quickly make a stock of evenly sized square tiles that you can cut down into appropriately shaped smaller pieces to fit a design as you work on it. Notice how the edges of household tiles are glazed and look different from the clay exposed by the cut edges. You can use the uncut edges in your designs to provide a neat finish to "frame" a piece.

Cutting shapes

Most mosaic designs, even the most complex-looking, can actually be completed using a fairly small repertoire of basic shapes. It is worth practising cutting triangles, circles and more complex shapes so that you can quickly and accurately cut the tiles as you proceed with a design.

Tools

Fibretip pen or chinagraph pencil

Ruler

Wheeled tile cutters

Nippers

Template for drawing circles

Materials

Tiles of your choice

CUTTING TRIANGLES

Triangles are a simple and useful shape and are the obvious first shape to attempt to cut as they are made by simply halving a square tile. The triangle is a staple shape in mosaic designs as they can be easily accommodated within the simplest grid to give variety and movement to flat areas of a design.

1 Marking the tile
Use a fibretip pen or chinagraph pencil and a ruler or other straight edge to draw a diagonal line between opposite corners of a tile. This is your cutting guide.

2 Placing the cutters
Place one of the marked corners of the tile between the wheels of the cutters. (Only place about 6 mm [¼ in] of the tile in.) The wheels should bear down exactly on the line.

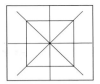

3 Making the cut
Now squeeze the handles of the cutters with increasingly firm pressure – don't "snatch" at them. The tile should split along the line you have drawn, neatly bisecting the single tile into two identically sized triangles.

4 Cutting smaller triangles
You can split the triangles you made by bisecting a tile in half again to give two smaller triangles. If you plan to do this, it is best to draw the necessary additional guidelines in advance – mark both diagonals of the tile as shown in the photograph. Then, having made the first split, follow the line that runs from the base to the peak of each triangle to split it in two again.

DRAWING OUTLINES

As you will see, when cutting all the shapes that follow in this section, it is recommended that you actually draw the outline of the shape and the cuts you need to make. This is not "cheating" but is a sensible way to ensure that you get accurate and consistently sized shapes, as well as reducing the wastage of expensive materials. A semi-permanent fibretip pen is ideal for drawing outlines – any residual marks can be easily cleaned off the surface of the tiles before you grout.

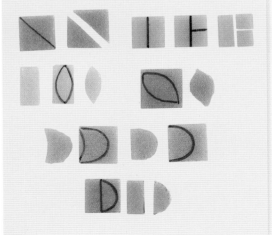

5 Even smaller triangles
For very fine work, you can even split the half-size triangles. Again, this is more easily done if you mark up your tile before making the first cut with the guides as shown in the photograph – draw both diagonals first, using the fibretip pen and straight edge, then draw vertical and horizontal lines to make a cross which runs through the centre point of the tile where the two diagonals cross.

CUTTING CIRCLES

The circle is a shape that – although it is used less often than the triangle – is often the centre of a key detail, so it is important to get it right. Cutting a circle relies on "nibbling" techniques; when you cut a tile to its approximate finished shape using basic splits, then use your nippers to gnaw away at the cut edges to create the final shape you want.

TILE GAUGE

If your design is going to require a number of identically sized shapes it is worth cutting batches of these in advance. Create a "tile gauge" on paper – an outline of the shape you want to create – then place every tile over this as you cut it to ensure they are all shaped and sized consistently. (Alternatively, use the first tile you cut satisfactorily – or any other template object you are using – as the gauge against which you compare every subsequent tile.)

It can be helpful to use a successfully shaped tile as a title gauge for further identical shapes.

1 Drawing the outline

The largest circle you can create from a single tile will have a diameter the width of the tile. To draw a circle freehand it may help you to draw centre lines vertically and horizontally to divide the tile into four, then to work on each quarter, drawing curves that connect edge to edge.

2 Using a template

An easier alternative to drawing a circle freehand is to find a circular shape that you can use as an outline – try different coins, buttons, washers or bottletops until you find your perfect circle. Once you have a template the right size, simply place the circle centrally on the tile and draw around it.

3 Starting to cut
Hold the tile between your thumb and forefinger and put one corner of the tile between the nipper blades so that they are just outside the line of the circle. Squeeze the nippers to cut off this first corner.

4 Nibbling
Rotate the tile a few degrees and follow the line of the circle with a sequence of "nibbling" cuts. Only try to cut off a tiny amount each time – no more than a millimetre – otherwise the tile is like to shatter. Continue around the tile until you have a circular shape. You can tidy up any irregularities by nibbling away any slight protrusions to achieve as near perfect a circle as possible.

5 Making smaller circles
You can create half-size circles by marking a single diagonal line on the tile with a fibretip pen, and then drawing a circle in each half. Make your first cut along the diagonal, exactly as if you were splitting the tile to make two triangles (see page 72). Nibble in from this first cut as before, to follow the outline of the circle.

6 Still smaller circles
Dividing the tile into quarters will allow you to create really tiny circles. At this size you will find it almost impossible to draw a template which means you will have to master drawing circles freehand. Start by splitting the tile down one centre line, then split each half in half again. Again, start the circle by splitting off one corner, and then nibble around the outline.

Andamento

"Andamento" is the term to describe the way the tiles flow within a mosaic. Andamento is the unique property of the mosaic art form: the one element that is present in no other comparable visual medium. The physical flow of the tiles — whether a smooth contouring around the design, or a jagged fill that breaks up or agitates the piece — is the extra dimension beyond shape and colour that the mosaicist has at their disposal to create the mood and effect of the finished piece. A successful andamento is the product of two factors. First: care and consideration at the planning stage. Second: while tiling, absolute precision and care in the cutting and positioning of the individual pieces so that they combine successfully into a single, organic entity.

The section on Opus (see page 100) gives examples of some of the classic andamenti employed by mosaicists since ancient times. But there are no hard-and-fast rules — you can adapt, mix, or ignore these rules in whatever way you feel works best. This picture of a swan mixes a number of different flows to create a variety of effects.

1 The body

The "core" of the swan is rendered with a naturalistic flow of parallel rows of tiles to emphasize the delicate curve of the neck into the body. The tiles are subdivided into groups of scalloped semicircular tiles that interlock to create the head and neck, and then merge with denser, rectangular shapes that give weight to the lower half of the body.

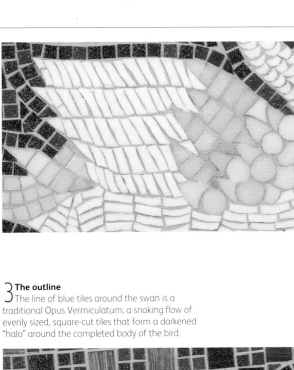

2 **Tile the wings**
The wings of the bird "blossom" out from the breast, with circular cuts of tiles which then flow into a more rigid herringbone that gives strength to the flight feathers. Note how different colours have been mixed with off-white and pearlescent tiles to add interest.

3 **The outline**
The line of blue tiles around the swan is a traditional Opus Vermiculatum; a snaking flow of evenly sized, square-cut tiles that form a darkened "halo" around the completed body of the bird.

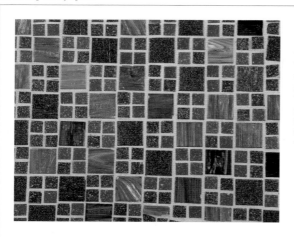

4 The checkerboard fill

The checkerboard background around the bird alternates whole tiles with "tile squares" made up of quarter-cut tiles (see page 86). This preserves the background rigidity that a checkerboard gives, but the smaller tiles add a depth and distance to this area where using only whole tiles would have produced a flatter, "deader" effect.

5 The waves

The wave forms used in the lower part of the picture give this area a quite separate, fluid feel – the parallel lines of tiles allow the eye to scan gently across the bottom half of the picture without interruption. The swan's reflection is created with areas of lighter toned tiles – but notice how the andamento continues regardless. It is important to cut the pieces of the waves so that they dovetail together, and the grout lines are even and harmonious allowing the andamento to flow uninterrupted.

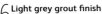

6 Light grey grout finish

The harmony of the tiling and the colours is best preserved with a light grey grout — too dark and it will fragment the body of the swan, too light and it will break up the unity of the background and the waves.

The direct method

The "direct method" is the most basic technique for laying mosaics and it is how most people start to experiment with this art form. It is called the direct method because you cut tile pieces and glue them directly onto the mounting surface.

Tools

Fibretip pen or carpenter's pencil

Nippers or wheeled tile cutters

Paintbrush or spatula

Cotton buds

Tweezers or toothpicks

IMMEDIATE RESULTS

The direct method has the advantage of being immediate – you can see the results as you work – unlike some of the more complex transfer techniques (see pages 168 to 177) where you are working back-to-front. However, this method is only possible where the location is suitable and allows you time to complete the piece.

Materials

MDF or similar

Vitreous tiles

White craft glue/PVA

Grout

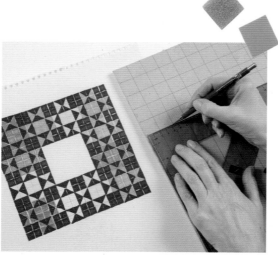

1 Transferring your design
Transfer your drawing to the surface you want to make the mosaic on, such as a suitably cut and prepared backing board (see page 20). For your first mosaic, use a piece of MDF or other similar board so that you can work comfortably and at your leisure on a suitable, well-lit work surface.

SEE ALSO
- -
Boards and backings, page 20

Transferring the drawing, page 128

2 Strengthening the outlines
Go over the drawing with a thick carpenter's pencil or fibretip pen (to enable you to see the design once you have started placing glue). Make notes if you need to; the surface will soon be covered by tiles and grout. You could even use markers to colour in the design and act as an accurate tiling guide (see "Colouring the grid", page 85).

3 Starting to place tiles
When you are happy with the design, start to cut and place tiles – without glue – into the outline of the design. Work on a small area at a time, checking that each tile piece fits. Move and rearrange pieces until they are just right, and don't be afraid to discard a piece that hasn't split exactly right or has any imperfections.

4 Leaving gaps for grout
Remember to leave gaps between the tiles for grouting later. These should be wide enough to accommodate enough grout to surround and support each tile piece, but should not be so wide that the finished design appears fragmented, with tile pieces floating in a sea of grout. You will learn the right balance through practice – the aim is to achieve an even, consistent grout line that seems to make the tiles flow as a unified whole.

5 Working on small areas

When you are happy with an area of tiles, move the pieces to one side keeping them in "formation". Use a brush or small spatula to spread white craft glue over the area where you want to stick the tiles. Only glue a small area that you can lay with tiles in five or ten minutes – before the glue becomes too tacky and lumpy.

6 Laying the glue

Remove any glue that becomes unworkable – cotton buds are ideal for this.

7 Placing the tiles

There is no "right" order in which to tile a mosaic – different rules apply to different designs. In this case it's logical to work from left to right but on other occasions it might be appropriate to start on detailed areas and then work around them. Move the tile pieces, one at a time, into the correct position. Use tweezers or a toothpick to nudge them into place. Check the gaps between the tiles as you go to make sure you are leaving a consistent grout line.

CHECKING THE END RESULT

When you have finished, take a step back and look at the piece objectively. Don't tolerate any wonky or mismatched tiles. Pry them out with an old screwdriver, cut fresh pieces, and reglue them. It is unlikely you will complete anything other than the simplest piece in a single sitting. If you stop for a break always scrape off any unused glue from the board and store the mosaic and any cut tiles where they will not be disturbed, such as in a cupboard or on a shelf. When the piece is complete leave it to dry thoroughly – for at least 24 hours – before starting to grout.

Simple fills

Simple fills that utilize uncut tiles or basic splits offer almost infinite possibilities of shape, texture and colour. However, planning the exact measurements of your design and drawing up a grid on the tiling surface are vital, in order to achieve the perfect result. Perhaps even more important than careful planning is the accuracy of your tiling – reproducing a strong, geometric design requires precise positioning and consistently spaced grout lines. Even the slightest deviation from the underlying grid will result in a noticeable imperfection in the final piece. The final grout colour is also very important in determining the appearance and flow of a pattern.

Tools
Ruler
Set square
Pencil or pen
Coloured fibretip pens
Paintbrush or spatula
Nippers or wheeled tile cutters

Materials
Graph paper
MDF or similar
Vitreous tiles

CHECKERBOARD FILLS

The simplest checkerboard patterns, which utilize uncut tiles, are a useful way of adding variety and interest to flat areas of a design. But make sure you plan how you will incorporate this type of fill. A square grid is completely rigid and it is particularly important that you consider what happens at the edges of such areas – you do not want to end up with tiny slivers of tiles or, conversely, rows of whole tiles from which you have to remove a tiny sliver.

1 Ruling up the grid

Once you have worked out how best to fit the checkerboard grid into your design (see "Fitting the grid to the design", page 86), rule up the grid, using a set square and long ruler to mark the lines.

2 Colouring the grid

Once you have drawn out the grid, it is a good idea to colour in the squares with fibretip pens as a tiling guide – it can be easy to get confused filling in even the simplest of checkerboards. If you have not decided on a pattern or colour mix, experiment first on some large-squared graph paper. Sketch a variety of ideas before committing them to your grid. You can find inspiration in all sorts of places: quilt patterns, decorative brickwork and paving designs are obvious geometric grids that work in similar ways.

3 Laying the tiles

You might find it easier when working with whole tiles to glue the backs of the tiles with a small brush, then place them onto your board, rather than gluing the surface of the board; this allows you to see the grid. (It is usually neater to glue the board first and then place the tile pieces.) Always place the whole tile into the same corner of each square, leaving space for the grout in the same position every time. Check for straightness using a ruler, sliding the tiles so that they are perfectly aligned along the edge.

FITTING THE GRID TO THE DESIGN

1 The grid you draw up for a simple checkerboard fill should be made up of squares the size of one tile plus an allowance for grout along one side and the top edge. So, if you are using a standard 20-mm (0.8-in) vitreous tile, make your grid of 22-mm (0.9-in) squares, giving you a consistent 2-mm (0.1-in) grout line. Don't start by simply drawing your grid from the first corner of the area that you want to fill. Instead, measure the width and work out how many whole squares will fit.

2 If there is any space left, divide this measurement by two and begin your grid of whole squares that distance from the edge. For example, to tile an area 170 mm (6.7 in) wide, you would begin tiling 8 mm (0.2 in) from the edge. Seven whole squares of 22 mm (0.9 in) = 7 x 22 (0.9) = 154 mm (6.3 in).

That leaves 16 mm (0.4 in) over. Halving that means that you will need an extra piece of tile 8 mm (0.2 in) wide each side to fill the whole width. Apply the same method to fit the grid into the height of the space.

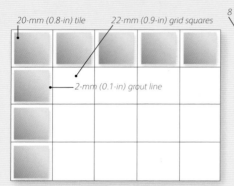

20-mm (0.8-in) tile   22-mm (0.9-in) grid squares

2-mm (0.1-in) grout line

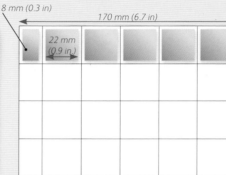

8 mm (0.3 in)

170 mm (6.7 in)

22 mm (0.9 in)

USING SPLIT TILES IN A GRID

You can add further variation to a simple square grid by splitting tiles — into half rectangles, quarter-sized squares or using a diagonal cut to create two triangles. This opens up a whole new layer of possibilities, as you can vary the placement of split tiles (for example, splitting the tiles at set intervals within an overall grid), combine split tiles of different colours within a single "cell" of the grid, or combine different splits within the overall design.

Remember that split tiles are "fatter" than a whole tile because each split requires the addition of space for grout. Therefore "half" and "quarter" tiles actually have to be cut slightly smaller to allow room for a dividing grout line and so that the edges do not protrude from their alignment with neighbouring whole tiles.

Wheeled-type tile cutters (such as "Leponitt") make splitting tiles for precision application much easier. They seem to produce far fewer "wrong" splits than conventional nippers. Try to get hold of a pair if you intend to produce lots of work using smaller geometric shapes.

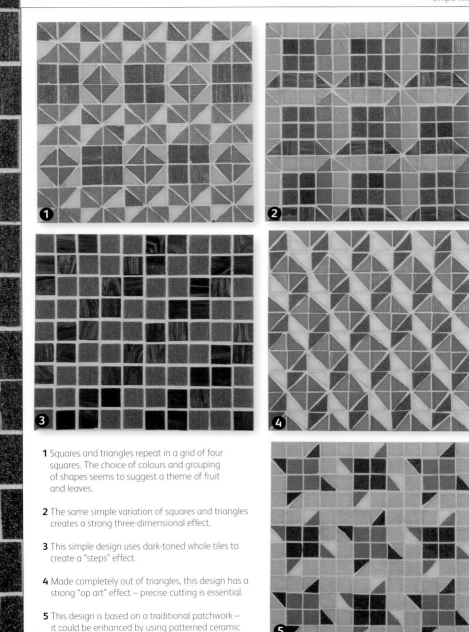

1 Squares and triangles repeat in a grid of four squares. The choice of colours and grouping of shapes seems to suggest a theme of fruit and leaves.

2 The same simple variation of squares and triangles creates a strong three-dimensional effect.

3 This simple design uses dark-toned whole tiles to create a "steps" effect.

4 Made completely out of triangles, this design has a strong "op art" effect – precise cutting is essential.

5 This design is based on a traditional patchwork – it could be enhanced by using patterned ceramic tile pieces.

Smalti

Smalti is the material in which Byzantine mosaics were made. It is produced in cakes, often about 30 cm (12 in) in diameter and is cut down from these into rectangular tesserae about 0.8 cm (⅓ in) thick and about 1.5 cm (⅔ in) long. Smalti is enamelled glass and has enormous intensity of colour. It is very expensive and not particularly easy to use. The glass is pitted with little holes and is traditionally left ungrouted because the holes fill up with grout, muting the vibrancy of colour. Smalti is only used for walls and small decorative pieces, since its fractured face and pitted body make it unsuitable for floors.

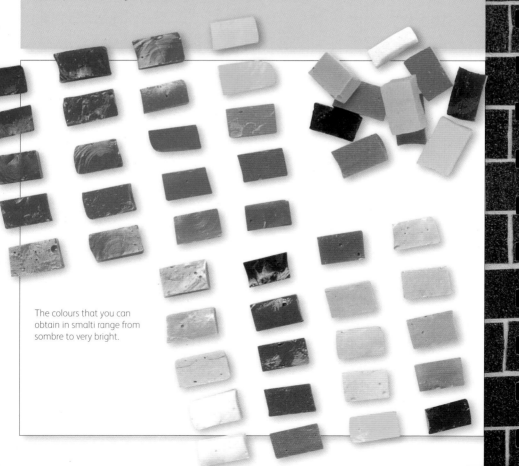

The colours that you can obtain in smalti range from sombre to very bright.

CUTTING SMALTI

Smalti comes in different grades, the lowest of which looks a bit like recycled glass and is difficult to cut accurately. Most commercially available material should be of better quality, but if you have problems making fine cuts, then try cutting from the top rather than the side.

Smalti can be cut either with wheeled tile cutters or with tile nippers. The fragments created are needle-sharp and dangerous. Clear away the glass dust with a brush, not with your fingers.

Smalti can be cut with a basic pair of tile nippers.

SMALTI MOSAIC
A simple design by Sue Majewski, rendered in smalti, in which two blends of colour collide to create strong vertical forms, while the "busy" fill adds interest and accentuates the horizontal bands running across the picture.

Tessellations

A tessellation is a pattern that can be repeated infinitely in two dimensions, in which each repeat fits perfectly against its neighbours without overlapping or leaving any gaps in between. Tessellations vary from the very simple – such as the much-used "checkerboard" fill (see page 84), to highly complex patterns.

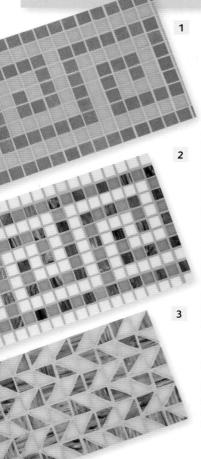

1

2

3

TRADITIONAL TESSELLATIONS

Tessellations have been used by the artists and craftspeople of different cultures for many thousands of years. Designs that use tessellating shapes have been a particularly strong feature of Islamic art, which has a graphic, rather than figurative, tradition. All the groups of tessellations "discovered" by modern Western mathematicians have been shown to be present in the tilings and mosaics of the Alhambra, the Moorish palace in Spain, which was built between the ninth and fourteenth centuries.

1 and 2 Variations on the classic "key" design.

4 A zigzag tesselation ideal for use as a border.

3 A simple split square grid enhanced by alternating the colours used.

5 Squares and triangles used to produce a striking geometric effect.

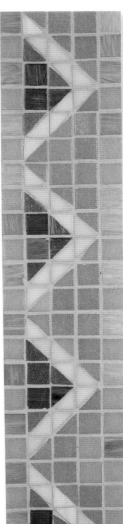

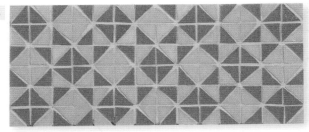

USING TESSELLATIONS

Tessellations are strong designs which are best rendered simply and boldly in their own right. Using anything but the simplest of tessellations within other designs risks introducing a distracting if not overpowering element.

Have a go at tiling a tessellation as a decorative panel, tray or tabletop. Follow the same rules as for the simple fills (see pages 84 to 87): plan your design on squared paper first, transfer the design to your surface as accurately as possible, and use a straight edge to keep the tiles and the repeats perfectly aligned.

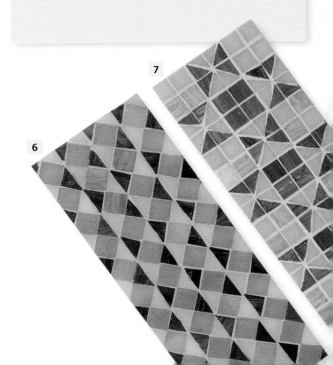

6 Here, alternating the colours of each section produces a secondary tesselation effect on top of the tile grid.

7 A variation on a traditional Roman design.

Borders

Border designs are useful for providing interest to large plain areas – for example as a strip running through an area of tiled wall. Patterns can also be used to "frame" a design, enlarging a piece and giving it more presence, as well as defining a neat and clean edge.

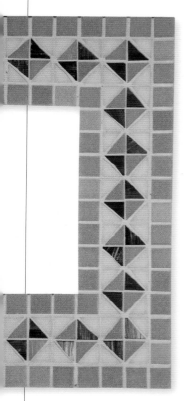

PLANNING BORDERS

You do need to plan borders carefully so that the design and the border work together in terms of size and colour. Every pattern has a frequency or "repeat" which is the physical length – the number of grid-squares – before the pattern starts again. For example, the pattern on the left has a repeat every two squares. If you wanted to use a patterned border to frame a picture then the width and height of the picture would have to be a multiple of the border pattern repeat – if not, one of the repeated sections of the pattern would be

TWO BORDER DESIGNS
Left: this border enhances a simple design with a strong differentiation of colour in the tiles chosen. Right: further embellishment to this basic design is added through splitting the inner and outer border of squares into rectangular pairs.

incomplete, ruining the
flow and appearance of the
whole piece.

The pattern-repeat
rule applies even to the
simplest border pattern
– two alternating colours, for
example – in this case the
repeat would be two squares.
To surround a picture with
a single band of alternating
coloured tiles, the perimeter
would have to contain an
even number of squares.
However, if you wanted the
frame to be symmetrical
– with the same coloured tile
in every corner, and opposite
tiles always of the same
colour – then the sides of
the frame would need to be
an odd number of units. Test
this by doodling on graph
paper to understand the
different patterns produced
by having sides containing
odd and even numbers.

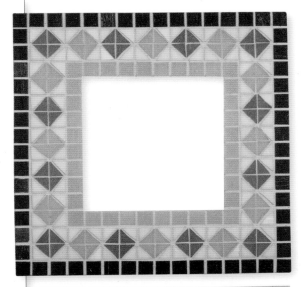

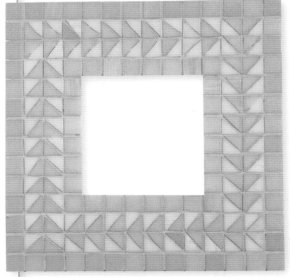

BORDER DESIGNS
Top: a frame motif based on a simple square grid but using
diagonal splits to create a diamond pattern. Bottom: a border
of split tiles creates a "running arrow" motif.

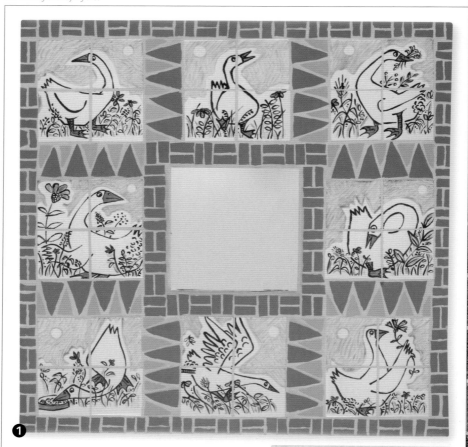

1

1 Here, scenes of a goose, inspired by Roger Duvoisin's *Petunia, Beware!*, have been painted across patterns of four tiles, and the scenes then arranged around the border. Ceramic tiles shaped into small rectangles and tall triangles have then been used to fill in-between the scenes.

2 This design uses patterned tiles to illustrate a scene of children and animals. Mirror glass has also been used for the chidren's faces. This would be a great piece for a child's bedroom.

2

3 For this design for a mirror frame, shaped tiles, painted to look like roses and leaves have been combined with a simple grid infill and some more painted tiles on the outer and inner edges.

4 For this border, hand-painted tiles have been combined with a crackle infill of tiles to create an interesting frame for a mirror.

3

4

Shatter fills

Shatter fills can be used to give areas of a design an energetic feel. A shatter fill works in completely the opposite way to "classical" mosaic fills where the grout lines flow neatly and continuously between tiles. In a shatter fill there is no such continuity – the grout lines run into and across each other, creating a jagged, disjointed feeling. Obviously this sort of effect needs to be used in a considered way. For many designs, only a flowing fill will work; a shatter fill should be used sparingly, so that the design is not submerged under the "noise" of the tiling.

Tools
Pencil
Nippers
Paintbrush

Materials
MDF
Ceramic tiles
PVA
Grout

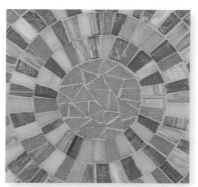

A shatter fill is often best attempted using household tiles. These allow a greater variation in the size of the pieces you can cut, making the finished effect more disjointed. You will also find these tiles easier to nibble down into snugly fitting pieces – smaller vitreous tiles are much harder to shape in this way.

USING A SHATTER FILL
In this example, the same motif has been filled using the same tile colours but with radial and shatter fills applied to different areas of the design in each case. The effect is very different – the one above creates a strong, radiant effect that extends to the edge of the picture, whereas in the version beneath the shatter fill creates a noisy background very separate from the centre circle.

1 Draw up your design
Transfer your drawing to the tiling area/backing board in the usual way. As well as marking up the colours for each area, think carefully about which type of fill will be suitable for which area of the design.

2 Tile the "regular" fills
This wave design consists of bands of flowing square tiles, interspersed with wider bands of shatter fill tiles. Cutting and gluing the square tiles first helps by giving a physical boundary to fit the irregular tiles of the shatter fill into.

3 Create shatter fragments
Don't be fooled by the apparently random nature of the tiles in a shatter fill – it is in fact very difficult to cut and fit the pieces together neatly and consistently. As with all fills, you want even gaps between tile pieces, so your cutting must be very accurate, with each individual piece cut to exactly fit. Begin by making a stock of roughly cut pieces and start placing them on your work surface and moving them around to fit.

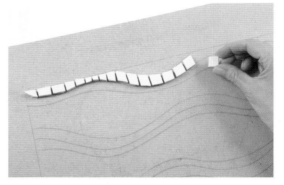

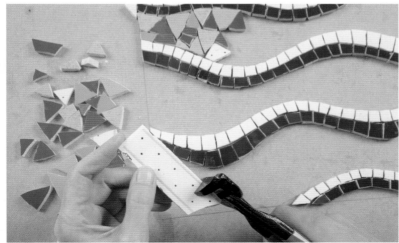

4 Treat the pieces like a puzzle
Don't glue anything down until you have worked out the way a whole area of tiles will fit together. Nibble at tiles to get them to fit together and avoid the temptation of using ever smaller pieces to fill any remaining "holes".

5 Grout and finish
Grout and clean the finished mosaic in the usual way.

CRAZY CACTUS
This design utilizes a shatter fill to accentuate the spiky
quality of the subject matter, then surrounds this with
a contouring fill to provide a calmer background that
emphasizes the outline of the cactus.

Opus

The word "opus" is used in mosaics to describe the different ways in which tiles can be laid. The different opera are like different rhythms that cause tiles of exactly the same shape and colour to have a very different impact within a design depending on how they are laid. The examples on these pages demonstrate some of the main "classical" opera being used to complete the background of the same design so that you can appreciate the differences between each one.

Opus regulatum

Opus tessellatum

Opus palladianum

Opus vermiculatum

Opus classicum

Opus circumactum

OPUS REGULATUM

This may look like the easiest way to lay tiles – a simple checkerboard pattern. In fact, to keep the rows and columns of the background in straight lines requires very careful cutting of the tiles so that the design can be accommodated without bunching of the tiles and maintaining even grout lines. It can be particularly difficult to take out small pieces from a single tile to accommodate extrusions within the design.

OPUS TESSELLATUM

Opus tessellatum is similar to opus regulatum, but the tiles are lined up in alternating rows – rather like the effect of bricks in a wall – with each tile centred neatly above the joint between the two tiles below. Like the regulatum, this opus lends a sense of stillness and solidity to a design.

OPUS PALLADIANUM

Sometimes referred to as "crazy-paving" fill, this opus gives a busy, restless feel to a flat area as there are no soothing lines for the eye to follow. This is a deceptively tricky fill to complete. Every piece needs cutting to fit and you should seek to keep pieces evenly sized — you cannot make do with broken bits and pieces jumbled together. Work on a fairly large area at a time, checking that everything fits together, repositioning pieces as necessary, before you start gluing pieces down.

OPUS VERMICULATUM

This opus is used to outline an element within a design and consists of evenly cut pieces of tile that snake alongside the edge of the element (the word comes from vermes, Latin for "worms"). The outline is sometimes executed in a lighter colour than the surrounding background to emphasize the halo effect.

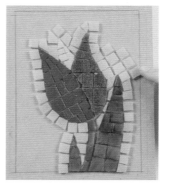

OPUS CLASSICUM

Opus classicum combines the flow of opus vermiculatum with the solidity of opus tessellatum.

OPUS CIRCUMACTUM

Opus circumactum is a fill pattern that, as well as being seen in mosaics, also appears in the laying of old cobbled streets. Each section of the fill is laid in a fan shape, with the different sections overlaying and butting against each other in a similar pattern to fish scales. The effect is a relaxed, undulating surround to a design.

Tiling three-dimensional surfaces

You can overlay any number of three-dimensional surfaces with mosaics to give them a new interest. Terracotta flowerpots and planters, for example, are relatively easy to work on as their porous surface provides a good "key" for cement and tile adhesives.

Materials

Three-dimensional object
PVA
Cement-based tile adhesive
Tiles
Grout
Paint
Clear varnish

Tools

Paintbrush
Plastic squeegee
Toothpicks
Rubber gloves
Sponge

MOSAICING ON A THREE-DIMENSIONAL SURFACE

You will need to work on quite a small area at a time, keeping that part of the object horizontal until the adhesive has set. You will also find that you can improvise temporary support for tiles while they set using masking tape, clingwrap or other materials.

1 Choose your object
When considering a three-dimensional object for a mosaic finish, the most important thing is the material it is made of. You need a fairly porous surface that will accept your adhesives and grouts. Avoid materials like glass or plastic which provide no "grip" or worse, as in the case of some plastic, is flexible. No matter how hard you try to stick them down, these materials will shed the tiles quickly.

2 Prime your surface
The bowl in this example is made from wound bamboo. Priming its surface with slightly watered PVA gives the cement or tile adhesive further encouragement to form a strong, permanent bond.

3 Work on a small area at a time

Only apply as much cement/adhesive as you can work on in a period of ten minutes or less. This is to avoid the grout drying out and becoming unworkable – if this does happen, scrape the waste off and discard it.

4 Use the shape of the object

The logical place to start this mosaic is from the centre – you then build the design upwards and outwards in rings – the tile pieces have nowhere to slide under the effect of gravity. Here, cement-based tile adhesive/grout has been used and the mixture kept fairly stiff to ensure that pieces do not slip.

5 Work outward

Cutting this design is like working on any circular motif – you will need to "dovetail" the pieces – that is, tapering each piece to fit neatly together and testing that they fit before gluing them. Work outwards, a ring of tiles at a time. On deeper bowls, with steeper sides, you may need to cut the tile pieces smaller to avoid a stepped look.

6 Grout by hand

When the design is complete, apply the grout. A tile squeegee will only work on a very curved surface if it is both relatively narrow and made of a very pliable material. Sponge off the excess grout and leave to dry. This bowl was painted on the outside with a suitable matching colour – you could also add a further protective layer of clear varnish to the outside.

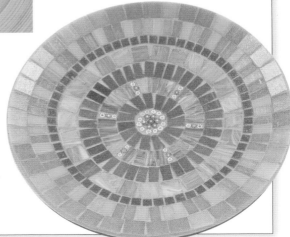

Shaping wood

You can further enhance your mosaic designs by shaping the baseboard using a jigsaw or router. MDF is a material that is easy to work using this method; it is soft and does not splinter or produce rough edges when cut. There are two important health and safety considerations to bear in mind when shaping MDF. First, make sure you wear a dust mask and eye protection. Second, if using an electrical tool, always make sure that there is a circuit breaker between the tool and the mains supply – if by accident you cut into the cable, the tool is immediately isolated, preventing electric shocks.

Tools
Thick pencil or fibretip pen
Clamps
Jigsaw
Router
Router bits
Fine sandpaper

Materials
MDF or similar
PVA
Tiles
Grout
Acrylic paint

CUTTING SHAPES WITH A JIGSAW

Electrically powered jigsaws are now available quite cheaply from DIY stores. You can use them to cut your baseboard into a variety of shapes – anything from a simple geometric design to the more complex outline of a bird or animal.

1 Draw a strong outline
Use a thick carpenter's pencil to draw your outline – this will enable you to see it more easily underneath the sawdust that is produced as you cut. Use clamps to hold the board in position so that it overhangs your workbench before you begin to cut. Check underneath to make sure you know where the edge of the workbench begins – you need to take care not to cut into the workbench itself. In most cases you will have to stop several times to reposition the board so that different parts of the design are overhanging the workbench and can be cut with the saw.

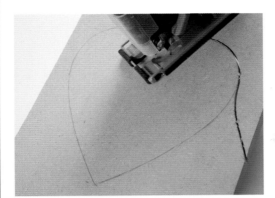

2 Cut into the board from an outside edge

Begin by cutting into the board from an outside edge, gently curving the cut so that you hit the drawn outline from a shallow angle. You can only change the direction of the cut through following a curve – if you cut in at too sharp an angle you will not be able to turn the saw blade to accurately follow the design.

DON'T RUSH

Work at a steady pace; if the saw has a speed setting then turn it to a low speed. Don't let the saw run away with you, and pause every so often to check your progress by releasing the power trigger but leaving the saw standing with the blade in the cut. Brush away any build-up of sawdust and check underneath to ensure that the blade is not cutting too near the work surface. Check also that the cable is clear of your cut line, before you resume your cut.

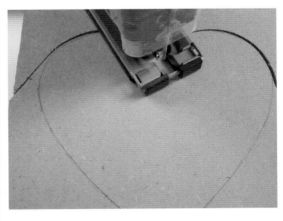

3 Cut in from different starting points

It is nearly always impossible to just follow the outline of a shape, to cut it out with a single cut. Any sharp angles in the design can only be cut by approaching the "elbow" of the angle with two separate cuts. Cut off any large pieces of waste as you progress. When the shape is cut out, clean up any rough edges with fine sandpaper, then seal and prepare the board by painting it with diluted PVA glue.

USING A ROUTER

A router is a specialist woodworking tool that allows you to hollow out areas from the surface of a piece of wood. With a router you can cut shapes from your baseboard into which you can set tiles so that their surface is flush with the surface of the board. This "inlaid" effect gives a very neat appearance to the tiled areas as the edges of the tiles are hidden. The surrounding board can then be painted to complement the tiles.

SELECT THE CORRECT ROUTER BIT

A router works by rotating a bit with sharp surfaces at high speed. Depending on the design of the bit, the router can cut both downwards and sideways into the wood as it is moved along the surface of the board. You should use a simple bit that leaves a neat vertical edge to the hollow it cuts – avoid the fancy-shaped bits intended for cutting decorative mouldings and other edges.

USING THE ROUTER

Routers are quite complicated to use, and require some practice, particularly if you are using them freehand, as in the following example. It is possible to buy templates – usually made from clear plastic – that act as a guide to the router. However, most of the available designs tend to be a little small for mosaic purposes. If you want to create an inlaid design using a router you will need to select a thick board so that you can hollow out areas without weakening it.

1 **Draw up your design**
A router will produce lots of dust so make sure the outline of your design is well emphasized by using a strong pencil or fibretip pen line.

2 Set the depth of the router

A router has a plunger mechanism that allows the bit to bite into the wood – there is a depth setting guide to control how deep the bit is allowed to go, and thus the depth of the hollow it creates. You should set the router to go to a depth equivalent to the thickness of the tiles you are using, plus an allowance for the thickness of the adhesive you will be using. For standard vitreous tiles you might set a depth of no more than 4 mm (⅛ in); for millefiori or thicker tiles you will need a greater depth.

3 Cut around the outline

With the marked-up board firmly clamped to a stable work surface, place the router in the middle of an area you want to cut, switch it on, then when the bit is at full speed, gently push the bit into the wood to begin cutting. Once the bit reaches the depth you have set on the guide you can lock it at that depth. Start to move the router sideways toward the outline of the design. At the point at which the rotating bit is about to eat into the outline, change the direction of movement so that you follow the line, keeping the edge of the bit as close to the line as possible. Follow the outline all the way around so that you have a routed path around the edge of the hollow you want to create.

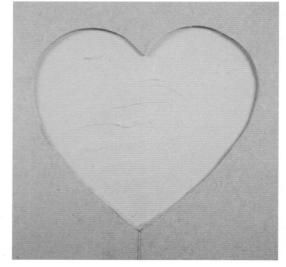

4 Rout out the centre of the shape

Now go back to your starting point, and moving the router from side to side, slowly remove all the "waste" from within the routed outline. Work methodically, eating into the wood you need to remove one bit at a time. The wood immediately around the area you are routing acts as a support for the base of the router, so as you remove more wood you cannot go back and clean bits up that you miss. You must thoroughly rout a small area before moving on to the next one.

5 Clean up and tile

Remove any rough edges from the cut area using sandpaper, then seal the MDF and tile as normal. At the end you can grout between the tiles, clean up and then when thoroughly dry, paint around the tiled area.

COMBINING TECHNIQUES

In this piece, only the heart in the routed area has been mosaiced – the rest of the detail in the design has been painted. The end result is a pleasing combination of the different materials.

USING MILLEFIORI

This piece combines three techniques. The heart shape was cut from a piece of MDF using a jigsaw; a second, smaller heart was then drawn on the central section of the board which was then routed to accommodate millefiori tiles. When using millefiori, the routed area needs to be much deeper than it is for other tile types, so measure some of the millefiori first to establish the depth needed. The picture around the heart is hand-painted using acrylic paints. In this example the millefiori tiles have not been grouted, instead the base of the inner heart is painted the same background colour first. The tiles are then packed into the routed area as densely as possible and glued in place with PVA.

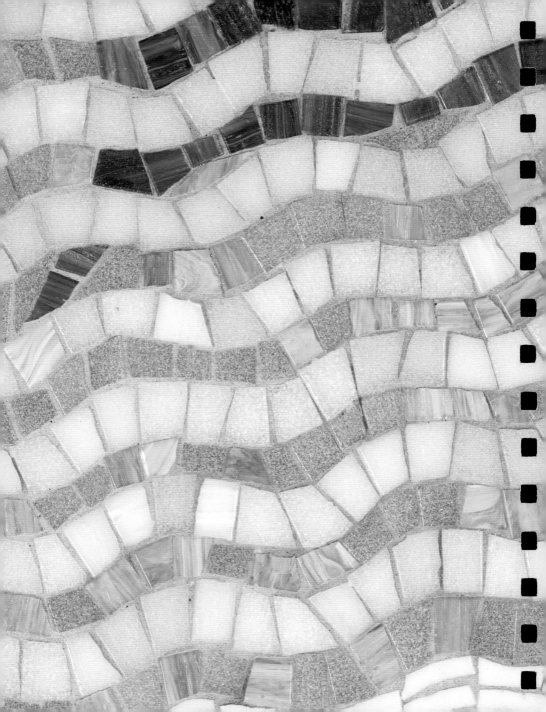

Planning and design

Turning a simple drawing into an accurate working "blueprint" for a full-sized mosaic can be made easier using traditional techniques as well as by exploring the possiblilities offered by newer technologies. This section looks at the traditional ways to scale up a drawing and how computers can be utilized to create quite different types of designs.

Scaling a drawing using a grid

If you have drawn a design for a mosaic – or found a picture that you would like to turn into a mosaic – then you will probably need to scale up the original to a larger size. There are a number of ways to do this – the traditional way is known as the "grid" method.

USING THE GRID METHOD

The grid method of scaling requires you to draw two grids: one of smaller squares, which you will place over the original; the other of larger squares which you will use as a guide to help you copy the original.

Tools

Sharp pencil

Eraser

Long ruler

Set square

Calculator

Materials

Clear acetate, tracing, or layout paper

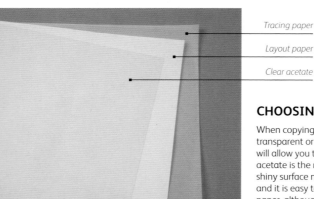

Tracing paper

Layout paper

Clear acetate

CHOOSING YOUR MATERIALS

When copying a drawing you need to use a transparent or translucent tracing material which will allow you to see the design underneath. Clear acetate is the most transparent material, but its shiny surface means you must use special pens and it is easy to smudge the drawing. Tracing paper, although not completely transparent, is probably easier to use as you can work with a pencil and erase any mistakes. Thin layout paper is an acceptable alternative, though it is more opaque than tracing paper, making it difficult to clearly see details, especially on photographs.

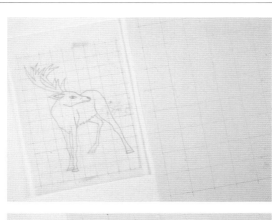

1 Drawing the original grid

Tape the original to a flat surface, and cover it with a sheet of tracing material slightly larger than the image all around. Measure the image with your ruler and work out the size of the grid squares you will need. (Aim for a grid consisting of between 10 and 15 squares along the longest side.) Use a set square to draw each vertical, then measure and mark the remaining horizontal lines of the grid.

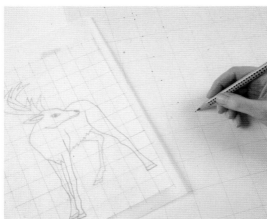

2 Drawing the enlarged grid

Now make the grid on which to create the enlargement. If you have a pre-cut board or wall area begin by measuring its width. Divide this measurement by the number of horizontal squares in the original grid to give you the size of the squares of the larger grid. Draw up the larger grid to the same number of squares wide and high as the small grid. Choose one of the main features in the original design, then mark the corresponding place in the enlarged grid with a dot. Transfer each line in turn, carefully marking a dot on the larger grid wherever a line crosses the feature in the original grid.

3 Joining the dots

When you have finished marking all the dots, join them up to reproduce the lines from the original. Check that the original and the copy look identical – with longer lines it is easy to miss a square and put a dot on the wrong line in the grid. (Numbering the squares along the bottom and sides of both grids can help you make sure you are in the right place each time.)

WORKING OUT THE SCALE OF AN ENLARGEMENT

1 Measure the longest side of the original and the length you want this side to be enlarged to.

2 Divide the enlarged measurement by the original measurement: this gives you the factor of enlargement.

EXAMPLE:

- Width of original: 15cm (6 in)
- Width of enlargement: 75cm (30 in)
- Factor of enlargement: 75 ÷ 15=**5** (30 ÷ 6=**5**)

The factor is the amount by which you must multiply any measurement from the original to find out the size it will be on the enlargement.

For example, if the original is 120 mm (4.75 in) high, the enlargement will be 120 (4.75) x **5** = 600 mm (23.75 in) high.

If you chose an original grid of 10-mm (0.4-in) squares, then the grid for enlargement would be made up of 10 (0.4) x 5 = 50-mm (2-in) squares.

ENLARGEMENT BY PERCENTAGE

Sometimes an enlargement is given in percentage terms. For example, if you use a photocopier to enlarge a drawing (see page 120) you might need to know the percentage value of the enlargement. You can find the percentage by multipying the factor of enlargement by 100. So, enlarging a drawing by a factor of 5 could also be expressed as a **500%** enlargement.

EXAMPLE:

A drawing in a book is 90 mm (3.5 in) wide. If you want to enlarge it on a photocopier to be 360 mm (14 in) wide you would calculate the percentage enlargement to use as follows:
360 ÷ 90 (14 ÷ 3.5) = **4** x 100 = **400%**

USING A LIGHTBOX

If you have access to a lightbox it can help make the tracing and scaling process much easier – a lightbox is like a translucent table top which shines light through the original drawing, making it more visible on the surface of the tracing material.

You can always improvise by taping your original drawing and the small grid onto the inside of a brightly lit window or glass door to get a similar effect as a lightbox.

1 Tape down the original
Use clear tape or masking tape to hold your source picture in place.

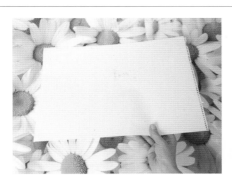

2 Position your drawing paper
Tape the paper you want to make the copy on over the top of the original.

3 Turn on the lightbox
The lightbox produces a strong but even light which allows you to clearly see the original beneath the paper. The advantage of the lightbox is that you can more clearly see the detail within darker areas, or within areas of similar tone, which are not always visible to the naked eye, even when using tracing paper.

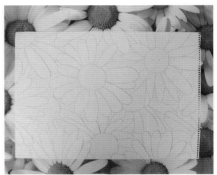

4 Trace the design
Use a sharp pencil to copy the design onto your drawing paper. When working from a photographic original like this, copy the main elements of the design – in this example the flower centres and petals. Don't be tempted to fill in all the detail which would overcomplicate the drawing and make it unsuitable for mosaic.

5 Check the finished drawing
Switch off the lightbox and check that you have not missed anything out in your finished tracing.

SEE ALSO

Scaling a drawing with a photocopier, page 120

Transferring the drawing, page 128

Scaling with a pantograph

A pantograph is a very simple but effective tool that allows you to trace around a design to produce an enlarged copy without having to draw grids or trace overlays. A pantograph consists of an extended parallelogram of hinged wooden or plastic rods. You can buy a pantograph fairly cheaply from an art store – or alternatively you can make your own.

USING A PANTOGRAPH

A pantograph has three elements: a fixed pivot – usually a screw – about which one corner of the pantograph rotates; a pointer which is used to trace round the original drawing; and a pen or pencil which, as the pantograph arm moves, creates the enlarged drawing.

Tools

Pantograph
Drawing pins
Masking tape
Pen or pencil

Materials

Large sheet of paper

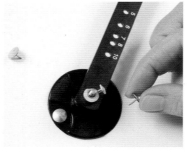

1 **Positioning the pantograph**
Securely fix the pantograph to a flat surface using pins, tape or whatever is suitable for the particular design of pantograph.

2 **Securing the original**
Use masking tape to securely fix the original drawing under the pointer.

SEE ALSO
- -
Scaling with a photocopier, page 120

Transferring the drawing, page 128

Pantograph

3 Tracing around the outlines

Tape a larger piece of paper under the pen or pencil on the end of the pantograph's longer arm (having checked that it is big enough and placed correctly to accommodate the whole of the enlarged drawing). Holding the pointer exactly like a pencil, carefully trace around the outlines of the original drawing.

4 Adjusting the drawing arm

The copy will begin to appear on the larger sheet of paper. Work slowly, because any inaccuracies will be enlarged on the copy. Lower the pen or pencil in its holder if the line the pantograph produces is illegible. Use your hand to raise the pen or pencil off the copy when you want to move from one part of the original to another – this avoids distracting "drag" lines connecting different parts of the design.

5 Adjusting the scaling

Change the position of the linkages of the pantograph on the pointer arm and drawing arm to change the scale of the image produced.

SUPERSIZED ENLARGEMENTS

You can make really big enlargements of a design with a pantograph by making a first enlargement, then using this as the "original" from which to create a second enlargement. You may find that you will need to work on separate sheets of paper for each of the final enlargements, then assemble these into a single sheet afterwards using clear tape.

Scaling with a photocopier

Photocopiers are widely available to use for a small charge in libraries or print stores. Using a photocopier is a very simple way of enlarging an original drawing to the size you want the finished mosaic to be without any of the difficulties associated with using a grid to scale the design. If your design is very intricate, you will probably find it especially worthwhile to use a photocopier to produce your "final" artwork.

Tools	Materials
Thin fibretip pen	Original artwork
Ruler	Photocopy paper
Calculator	Clear tape
Photocopier	
Scissors	

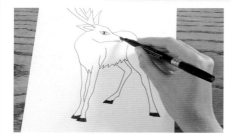

1 Strengthening the original

Depending on how big your finished design is going to be, it is likely you will need to enlarge your original drawing more than once. The copying process can degrade the design slightly at each step, particularly if the original was done in pencil or coloured crayon, so before starting it is worth using a thin, dark fibretip pen to go over the design and darken the outlines.

2 Work out the finished size

Measure the size of the board, or the area that the finished mosaic is to be stuck to, then measure your drawing. To work out the percentage, you will need to scale the drawing. First divide the longest measurement (the width if the design is "landscape", the height if it is "portrait") of the finished piece by the measurement for the corresponding dimension of the drawing. Multiply this number by 100 to get the percentage enlargement. For example, if the finished width of the piece is to be 500 mm (20 in) and the original is 200 mm (8 in), then the enlargement is: 500 (20) ÷ 200 (8) = 2.5 x 100 = 250 %.

3 Photocopying the original

Open the lid of the photocopier and place the drawing face down on the glass. Check where to position the original when making the enlargement. Enter the percentage enlargement you have calculated using the control panel on the photocopier. Some copiers have a maximum setting – for example 200 %, or even 141 %, which is the scale setting to enlarge an A4 (letter) piece of paper to A3 (tabloid). If so, make a first copy at the maximum setting.

4 Copying in sections

It is likely that not all of your drawing will fit onto one piece of paper when enlarged. Rotate the original in the photocopier and make a copy of the second part. You may need to do this more than once – in which case treat the original as four corners, each of which will need to be enlarged. If you have not been able to go as large as you wanted with the first copy, then copy the copies. You will probably have to change the scaling for the second copies to end up with the intended size. Measure the size of the interim copy. For example, the 200-mm (8-in) drawing in our original example would have ended up at 400 mm (16 in) if the photocopier allowed a 200 % enlargement. Perform the same calculation again to work out the next enlargement: 500 (20) ÷ 400 (16) = 1.25 x 100 = 125 %. You would need to copy each of the sections of the first copy using a 125 % setting.

5 Assembling the image

When you have copied and enlarged all of your first copies (again, you may need to make more than one copy of each sheet to fit everything in) lay all the drawings out on a large table or the floor to line the pieces up. Check that the image is complete, use scissors to cut away any borders, then use clear tape to join all the sections together. The enlarged drawing can be transferred by scribing with a soft pencil on the underside of the photocopy to create a carbon-paper effect.

Scaling with a scanner and projector

If you have access to "professional" computer equipment such as a scanner and an LCD projector of the type used to give business presentations, then enlarging just about any image is exceptionally easy, and all the labour of drawing grids can be avoided.

Tools

Photo editing program
Scanner
Projector
Pencil

Materials

Original drawing
MDF

1 Scanning your design

Take your original drawing and scan it into your computer in a suitable file format – one that can be opened in a photo editing program or imported into a word processing document. If your original is larger than the copy area of your scanner, then just copy a bit of the original at a time, rotating and copying each corner in turn.

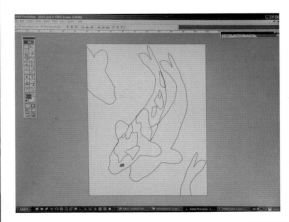

2 Using an editing program

Open the scanned image in a photo editing program. If you scanned the image in sections, you can combine the pieces together in the program, aligning each carefully with its neighbour. You can also use the software to clean up your drawing, adjust the brightness and contrast, and strengthen outlines.

3 Using the projector

Place the projector on a surface such as a table and turn it on, then project the design onto your mosaic baseboard, which should be hung or supported vertically against the wall. Adjust the design to the correct size by either using the projector's zoom facility if it has one, or by physically moving the projector nearer to, or further from, your baseboard.

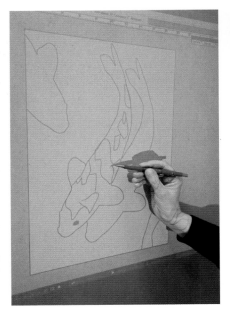

4 Drawing around the design

When you are happy that the scaling is correct, use a pencil to trace around the projected drawing onto the surface of the board. Mask the light from the projector occasionally to check that you are transferring everything – make sure you have a completely finished copy of the design before you move the projector as it is very hard to reposition everything at a later stage.

Designing with a computer

In the last decade, computers in the home have become common, giving many people access to computer drawing programs. While in the end there is no substitute to actually making mosaics in order to really understand the possibilities of the medium, computers can sometimes provide useful design assistance when exploring and testing ideas.

"PLAYING" WITH COLOURS

You can use a simple "paint" program on a computer to quickly try out different colour schemes for your mosaic designs, or to test different combinations of colours before cutting or gluing a single tile. With this type of program you can quickly fill whole areas of a design with flat colours to see which might work and which to avoid.

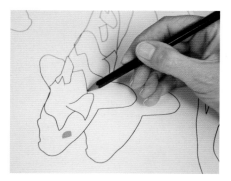

1 Draw up your idea
The easiest way to get your design onto a computer is to draw up your idea on an A4 (letter) size piece of paper – do the drawing in pencil first so you can make corrections, then when you are happy with it, go over it with a black fibretip pen to create strong outlines.

2 Scan the image
Now scan the image. You will have a choice of formats that you can save the picture as – choose a common format such as .jpg or .gif, because nearly every drawing program can open these files and work with them.

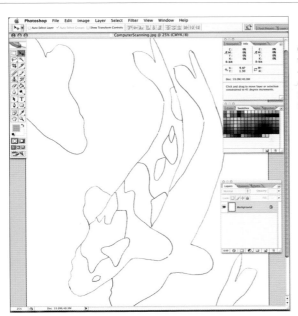

3 Open in a drawing application
Open up your image in a drawing application. Most computers come with a simple drawing package – photo editing software is also available to download on the internet – either as "freeware" or to use as a trial.

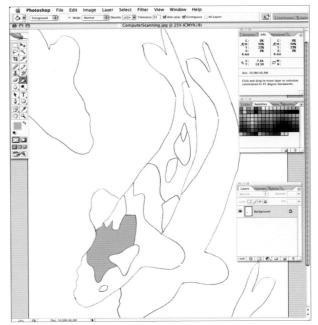

4 Fill areas of the design
The drawing program will usually have a "fill" tool – often represented by an icon of a tin of paint – which allows you to fill an area with a colour you select from the palette. Hold the tool over an area of the drawing to fill it with colour – the colour will "flood" as far as any containing outlines. This is why it is important that your drawing has strong lines separating the areas of colour.

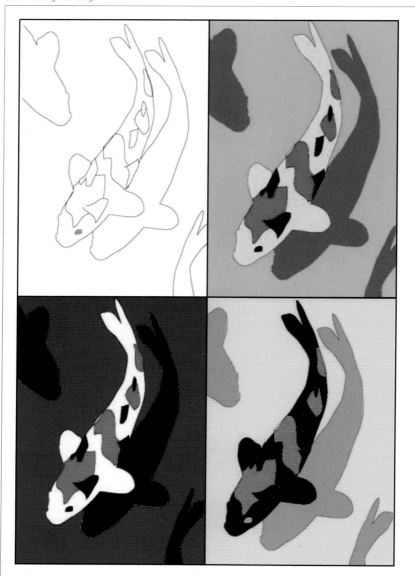

5 Experiment with colour combinations
You can use the fill tool to quickly produce different colour treatments of the same drawing.

MAKING A TILE GRID TO COLOUR

You can use the same method to design your own geometric patterns where you are planning to use a simple grid of tiles all of the same shape – for example, "quarter" tile squares, or triangles made by diagonally splitting whole tiles.

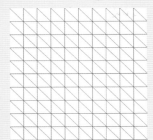

1 Creating the grid

Use a dark fibretip pen to draw your grid – in this example, the grid has been produced on the computer but you could produce a grid by strengthening the lines on an area of a sheet of graph paper. Scan the drawing and then open up the file in your drawing application.

2 Experiment with different patterns

As before, use the fill tool and different colours to experiment with different pattern repeats and colour combinations. If you are familiar with the software you should be able to create your own graph paper background using the line tools for a slightly neater result. There are also a number of mosaic creation websites on the internet where you can experiment with geometric grids and print the results.

Transferring the drawing

Once you have enlarged your drawing you will need to transfer it to the baseboard or other surface on which the mosaic is to be laid.

Tools
Soft broad pencil or chalk
Hard coloured pencil
Eraser

Materials
MDF or similar
Tape

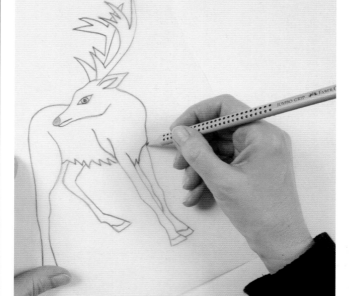

1 **Rubbing the reverse of the drawing**
Start by turning over the enlarged drawing on a flat surface. Use a soft pencil or chalk to rub heavily over the back of the drawing – concentrating on the areas where the lines are. Aim to leave a fairly heavy deposit of pencil or chalk on the reverse of the drawing. If you drew your copy onto a transparent tracing material you will find it much easier to follow the lines of the original; a lightbox is also useful for this purpose.

SEE ALSO

Boards and backings, page 20

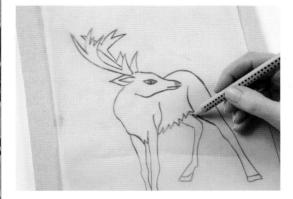

2 Scribing over the original

Turn the drawing the right way up and tape it in place on your tiling surface. Retrace the outline of the drawing – this time with a hard, sharp pencil or crayon. Use it almost like a scribing tool to press the pencil or chalk from the back of the drawing onto the tiling surface. (Using a hard coloured crayon has the advantage of showing you which parts of the drawing you have traced over.)

3 Removing the drawing

When you have traced over the whole of the enlarged drawing, peel away one corner so that you can check that everything has transferred. Go over any weak areas with a pencil to strengthen the lines. When you have checked the whole drawing – work in from a corner at a time to avoid moving it – peel the drawing off completely. Go over the work surface with an eraser to clean up any bad smudges, and make any final corrections. You are now ready to begin cutting and laying your tiles.

Posterization

"Posterization" is a technique for simplifying the number of tones in a photographic image. For the mosaicist it provides a method for turning a complex image into areas of flat colour which can be more easily rendered in the limited palette of colours or tones normally at your disposal in the form of tiles.

Materials

High contrast image
MDF or similar
White craft glue
Grout

Tools

Computer
Photo editing software
Scanner
Printer
Tile nippers or wheeled tile cutter
Small paintbrush

POSTERIZING WITH A COMPUTER

Many photo editing programs have a function that allows you to take any image and posterize it. Your source photograph could be a family snapshot (taken by a digital camera, or scanned into a computer), a digital image from the internet or a picture scanned into a computer from a book or magazine.

1 **Choosing a photograph**
Choose a strong image with areas of light and dark. Avoid images with lots of delicate details or subtle tones – all these will be lost in the process. A good test is to look at an image and half-close your eyes – if you can still decipher what is happening in the picture, then it is more likely to be legible after posterization.

Wrong choice
✗ No contrast
✗ Thin lines and detail
✗ Areas merge together

Right choice
✔ Strong contrast
✔ Strong outlines and bold shapes
✔ Distinct areas

2 **Open the photo editor**
Open the image in a photo editing program. (Scan the image into your computer first if the original is in printed format.)

3 Cropping the image
Look at the image and choose an area to concentrate on in "close-up". Use the software to remove – or "crop" – any parts of the image that are unnecessary.

4 Converting the image to grayscale
Turn the image into a black and white version by changing the mode of the picture to grayscale using a drop-down menu, or using the "Save as" function and selecting the grayscale option.

5 Despeckling the image
Most photo editing software has a "Despeckle" or "Remove noise" function which allows you to remove any fine texture from the image. Apply this filter and you will see how your picture appears to instantly soften. This is a useful first step to simplifying your image.

6 Posterizing the image
The "posterize" command allows you to set how many tones the image will be reduced to. For example, if you choose "2" an image will be converted to just black and white – normally the end result looks stark and bleached out, and whole areas of the image may be illegible.

7 Retain some tonal variation
Generally, choosing three, four, or five "levels" will give sufficient tonal variation to retain the shapes and features of objects within the picture.

8 Experimenting
As long as you keep a backup of your original image, you can experiment with different variations. As well as trying different posterizing settings, you can also try changing the contrast of the image and to see what result this has.

9 Printing and tiling

When you are happy with the result, try printing the image out. You will need to have access to a printer which allows you to enlarge an image across a number of sheets – known as "tiling" – in order to print your design at the size of the finished mosaic. Trim and fit the pieces together, then carefully glue them to a suitable baseboard. Begin tiling, laying the tiles directly on top of the glued-down printout. Start with the lightest colour.

10 Following the tonal areas

Use "nibbling" techniques to cut tiles of different tones to fit exactly the different areas of the printout. Interpret the edges of the tonal areas, trying to maintain the jaggedness of the posterisation.

FRAMING A PORTRAIT

A nice way of completing a portrait piece such as a posterization is to create a decorative picture frame. Design the frame in keeping with the picture within it – perhaps using metallized gold tiles to surround an "old master", for example. This posterized picture of Audrey Hepburn utilizes a suitable 1950s flower motif and a soft pink colour.

11 Completing the picture

When you have completed the lightest area, move onto the next darkest tone, and so on, finally finishing with the black. Grout with a mid-tone grey, clean up then admire the result from a distance.

REINTRODUCING COLOUR

When processing the image into tonal steps you need to work in grayscale mode. However, once you have done this and established the tonal divisions, there is no reason why you cannot go back to the image on your computer and try different colour combinations. Most photo editing programs have a "paint bucket" tool which allows you to flood areas that are the same colour or tone with an alternative colour. In this way, you can select a palette of three or four colours (perhaps choosing those for which you have tiles) and experiment with different colour variations. Print out the result on a colour printer and use it as a guide to help you produce a more colourful finished piece.

A naturalistic colour palette

An "Op art" colour palette

Mosaicization

"Mosaicization" is the process of simplifying a digital image into a grid of "tiles" of uniform size, with the colour and tone of each tile rendered as an "average" of the area of the picture it encloses. The effect is similar to using uncut square tiles to interpret the tones of a photograph. To mosaicize a photograph, all you need is an original in a digital format and a photo editing program with a pixelation or mosaic filter. You can use this technique to create a design from a computer which you can then print out and carefully tile over.

Tools

Computer
Photo editing software
Scanner
Printer
Tile nippers or wheeled tile cutter
Small paint brush

MOSAICIZATION FROM A PRINTOUT

The wonderful thing about a mosaicized design is that it uses whole tiles – you can scale your design to fit the tiles you have so that you do not have to cut even a single one. The end result has a mesmerizing impact. The difficult bit is producing the drawing the right size.

Materials

High contrast image
Glue stick
MDF or similar
White craft glue

1 **Choosing an original**
Find a suitable image to use – either a digital original, or a picture scanned from a magazine or book. It will need to be a "high contrast" image with strong areas of light and dark tones. If the image is too delicate, the mosaicization process will make it illegible.

2 Cropping the picture

Open up the image in a photo editing program. You can make the image stronger by cropping the picture – if you are processing a face, for example, a close crop of the eyes and mouth is very effective.

3 Converting the image to grayscale

If you are working with a colour original, turn the image mode of the photograph to "grayscale".

4 Applying the mosaic filter

Depending on your software, the mosaic or pixelate effect may exist as a filter or plug-in. The main control you have is in varying the size of the tiles. Experiment with this to see the end result. Each square in the picture corresponds to a tile in the finished piece, so count the squares and multiply the numbers by your tile size to work out how big the end result will be.

5 Reducing the tones

The mosaicized picture you have produced will contain many – perhaps hundreds – of tones of grey. Use the program's posterization filter (see page 131) to reduce the image to black, white and three or four shades of grey. Each of these tones will be matched to the tone of a tile in the finished mosaic.

6 Enlarging the design

Now that you have the image looking like a proper mosaic you need to enlarge it to become a full-size working drawing you can fix to your tiling surface. To work out the finished size, find out how many tiles high and wide it is, and multiply these numbers by the size of the tile, remembering to add extra to each for grout. Resize the image and print it out, making sure that the printer is set to print at "actual" size (so the images will be "tiled" across several sheets of paper).

Position the sheets carefully on the baseboard, then glue and press them firmly to the surface using white craft glue.

7 Tiling in sequence

Select and sort tiles into batches for each of the tones represented in the picture. Then begin gluing down the tiles onto the surface of the paper, making sure you align each row accurately, and choose tiles of the correct tones. (Don't worry about the printout creating a layer of paper between the board and the tile backs – providing you do not use a thick card and glue the printed sheets down properly, the tiles will stay firmly in place.) Continue tiling until the whole piece is complete.

CUTTING BATCHES OF TILES
Wheeled cutters really simplify cutting a large number of quarter tiles. Cut a good batch of each tone so that you can work speedily and concentrate on accurately placing the tiles without the interruption of cutting more.

HALF-SIZE VERSION USING QUARTER TILES

You can produce a more delicate version of the image by using quartered tiles and scaling the printout to fit their dimensions. But beware – quartered tiles take up proportionately more space than the whole tile because you are adding an extra grout line. Scale your drawing accordingly, making each grid square the size of a quarter of a tile, plus a grout line at the top and side. Following the drawing on this small scale can be difficult. It can help to go over the glued-down printout with a rule and pencil to clearly establish the grid.

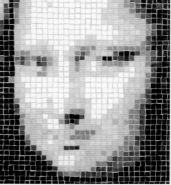

8 The finished piece
You could experiment with using a variety of colours and clashing tones to replace each of the tonal areas of the processed image.

FINISHING

You can either complete one tonal area at a time, or work from left to right a row at a time, selecting the correct tile for each grid square. Grout with a mid grey to hold the extremes of tone together, then clean up your work. You could add a mosaic "frame" to the picture, as suggested on page 132

5 Maximizing impact

Understanding how to combine colours
and tones to produce a range of effects
will help you to add an extra dimension
to your mosaic pieces. This chapter
introduces ideas and concepts used by
artists and designers down the centuries
to produce memorable results.

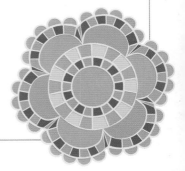

Colour

An introduction to some basic colour theory is useful – it will help you to understand how different colours will work when placed together, and therefore help your choice and organization of colours within a mosaic design to produce different moods and effects. Unlike paints and other artists' media, the colours in the mosaic "palette" are determined by the tile pieces – you cannot mix your own colours. The advantage with mosaics however is the purity and brightness of the colours available – mosaic designs often work best with a bold and decisive use of colour that plays to the strengths of the raw materials.

COLOUR WHEEL

The colour wheel organizes colours to show clearly how they interact with each other. The wheel places the three primary, or pure, colours equidistant from each other around the rim of the circle – red, blue and yellow. In between are the "secondaries" – the colours that result from mixing the primaries on either side – purple (red plus blue), green (blue plus yellow) and orange (yellow plus red). The wheel continues in this way, with more colour gradations created by the mixing of adjacent colours – so, for example, to one side of orange will be a "yellowish orange"; on the other side a "reddish orange".

If you work with colours close to each other on the wheel, the effect tends to be more harmonious. If you select colours from opposing sides of the wheel, then the effect is more clashing and discordant.

The colours you choose will depend on the design itself, the effect you want to create, and even on the context in which the piece will be displayed – for example a design made up of "harmonious" reds and oranges will look quite different when hung on a blue wall.

COMPLEMENTARY COLOURS

Complementary colours are colour pairs that belong to opposite hues on the colour wheel. When placed side by side, complementaries make each other appear brighter. The purest complementary pairs are red and green, blue and orange and yellow and violet.

Red

Warm

Purple

Orange

Blue

Yellow

Cool

Green

MOSAIC COLOUR WHEEL

The colour wheel illustrates some of the important rules of the way colours work when placed together. This colour wheel, has been created using mosaic pieces patiently sorted into primaries and secondaries. The end result shows how a mosaicist is always limited by the tiles that are available to them – because you cannot mix your own colours, there will always be gaps in the colour palette available to you.

Complementaries
Complementary colours, such as red and green, sit opposite each other on the colour wheeel.

Harmonious
Colours that sit next to each other on the colour wheel, such as red and orange, are harmonious.

SOME COLOUR TERMS

Hues
These are the pure colours described by names such as "red", "green", "purple" and "blue". Within each hue colours may be differentiated depending on their brightness or saturation – for example, "electric blue" – or the degree of lightness or darkness – for example "pastel blue".

Warm and cool colours
Colours are often described as warm or cool depending on their associations. Warm colours are generally thought of as the colours from red to yellow – including browns; cool colours include the hues blue and green, and also greys. Warm colours

are associated with energy, and seem to push themselves forwards within a design. Cooler colours are seen as more relaxed and soothing and tend to recede backwards into a design. These properties (which are as much a psychological or cultural response to a colour as opposed to a "scientific" property) are important considerations in the choice of tiles for any piece.

Tone
Tone is the degree of lightness or darkness of a colour. Two colours can be of the same tone, though of different hues – that is equally light or dark. (This idea can be easier to understand if you think of two tiles – one orange and

one green placed side by side. If the tiles were of the same tone they would appear identical in a black and white photograph.)

Contrast
Contrast describes the variation in hue or tone within an area of colour, a picture or a design. Where colours of opposite hues are placed against each other or where there is a variation between lightness and darkness then this would be described as "contrasting".

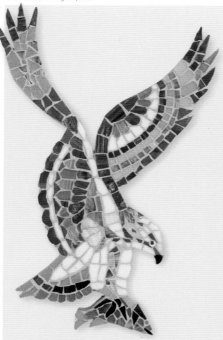

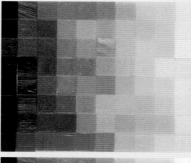

SEPIA TONES
This tonal picture of a diving osprey works by using a variety of warm brown and golden tones to give a complex but highly naturalistic tonal effect.

TONAL DIFFERENCE
Here, tiles have been laid out in vertical bands of the same tone. When the image is reproduced in black and white, you can see the tonal differences (and similarities) of the different tiles more easily.

TONE

"Tone" describes how dark or light a colour is. Two areas of different hues but of the same tone will appear closer together and more harmonious than areas of very different or contrasting tones. The tone of an object will appear to change relative to its surroundings – so the same tile surrounded by lighter or darker tiles appears to be of a different tone.

The easiest way to compare the tones of different tiles is to half close your eyes – this suppresses the hue of the tiles, and makes it easier to see the relative lightness or darkness of the different tiles. A black and white photograph achieves the same effect more accurately – completely removing the hue of the elements of a design and showing clearly the relative light and dark of the components.

Within conventional pictures, lighter tones tend to recede into the background and seem farther away, while darker, stronger tones appear to be more in the foreground.

Within mosaics, tone is perhaps the most important consideration when choosing grout. In most mosaic designs there will be a range of tiles of different colours. To hold the design together it is therefore best to choose a fairly neutral colour – typically a grey that will not clash with any of the tile colours – then darken or lighten it to a tone close to the majority of the tiles in the design. Grout of the same tone as the tiles will tend to hold the design together – a tone that is too dark or too light will tend to fragment the design (see examples on page 184).

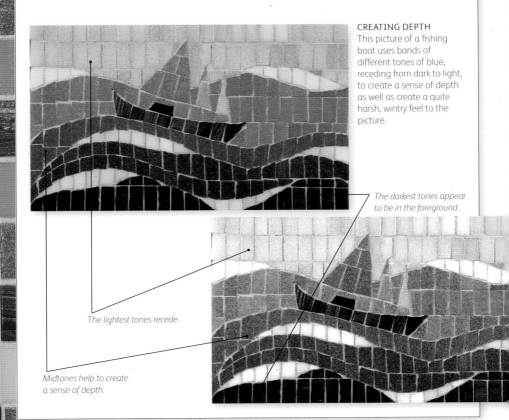

CREATING DEPTH
This picture of a fishing boat uses bands of different tones of blue, receding from dark to light, to create a sense of depth as well as create a quite harsh, wintry feel to the picture.

The darkest tones appear to be in the foreground.

The lightest tones recede.

Midtones help to create a sense of depth.

CONTRAST

Contrast is the difference in the colour and "brightness" of an object and its surroundings or background. The human eye is much more sensitive to these differences between things in its field of view than it is to the overall brightness or darkness of what it is looking at. Contrast is therefore very important in making elements of a picture or design stand out, or conversely, blend together.

TWO ROSES
A simple flower motif is here rendered in contrasting colours in two panels, which are symmetrical duplicates, with each half of the design a reverse of its opposite. Although identically sized, the yellow flower head appears bigger against a red background, than its darker counterpart on a light background.

STRIPED ELEPHANT

There are no tile pieces making up a conventional tile outline in this mosaic piece. The form of the elephant is created entirely by the contrast between the alternating stripes of black and white – the strongest colour contrast possible.

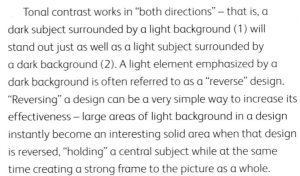

Tonal contrast works in "both directions" – that is, a dark subject surrounded by a light background (1) will stand out just as well as a light subject surrounded by a dark background (2). A light element emphasized by a dark background is often referred to as a "reverse" design. "Reversing" a design can be a very simple way to increase its effectiveness – large areas of light background in a design instantly become an interesting solid area when that design is reversed, "holding" a central subject while at the same time creating a strong frame to the picture as a whole.

Colour contrast is achieved by using the same principle of separation of areas of the design, but according to hue rather than tone. Here, the subject is strengthened by the colour of the background, even though they are very similar in tone (3). The most extreme contrasts are created using complementary colours (see page 146).

As with every colour effect, contrast should be considered as just one more tool that you can use – in different ways, and not on every occasion.

COMBINING COMPLEMENTARY COLOURS

Because mosaic tiles come in a range of such pure colours and are so "ready to use"
– with no hit or miss mixing of colours involved – you can experiment with different colour
combinations and effects before committing yourself with glue and grout. In fact, you
can try out any number of colour combinations for a design to see what works best.

One colour technique you should experiment with and understand is combining
complementary colours. These are colours that are opposite each other on the colour
wheel, which, when placed side-by-side, gain an extra intensity. You can use this technique
in simple geometric patterns, to give a vibrant, sometimes almost overpowering effect. But
you can also use complementaries more subtly, for example within illustrative pictures, by
using dark tones of complementary hues to make shadows around objects and elements.

THE "SHIMMER" EFFECT
This quadrant layout of circular motifs is
made up of blue and orange household
tiles which create the "shimmer" effect that
complementaries of the same tone produce
when placed next to each other.

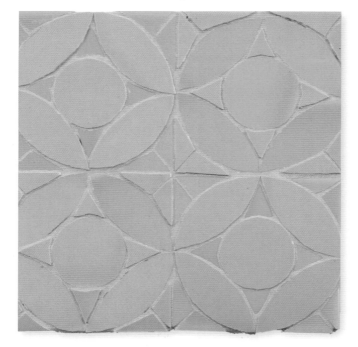

Bright yellow teamed with palest mauve makes the yellow stand out.

A strong red paired with very pale green causes red to advance.

COMPLEMENTARY SCHEMES

As well as choosing the right hue, the effect of complementary colour pairs can be increased depending on the closeness in tone of the two hues. The nearer they are, the more pronounced is the "zing" that their juxtaposition creates. But you can also use more "atonal" pairings, by utilizing tile contrast of light and dark tones to produce subtler effects. Alternatively, you can blend more natural colours that contain only a tint of each complementary, for example earthy browns and leaf greens. All the examples shown on the right are pairings of complementary colours which have very different end results.

Earthy brown and leaf green create a muted pairing.

Deep orange and blue together create a shimmering effect.

Yellow and very dark purple contrast with each other.

Orangey red and mint green.

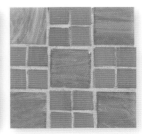

Darker shades of green and purple.

This light-toned blue interacts vibrantly with the bold orange.

Drop shadows

A "drop shadow" is really an artificial shadow that you can add to an object to give a three-dimensional effect. It can make an object appear to be resting on, or floating above, a background. Drop shadows around parts of a design are commonplace in computer graphics, but the same technique has been employed by signwriters for hundreds of years to make lettering stand out. It is a very simple technique that is useful for strengthening designs and highlighting key elements.

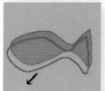

A drop shadow is most simply created by drawing around the outline of an object, then moving the outline down and to the side – the space in between the object and the "shifted" outline can then be filled in with a suitably dark colour to create a shadow.

Unlike a "natural" shadow – which is generally created by multiple sources of light, and distorted depending on the point of view – a drop shadow is highly stylized. However, you can make a shadow slightly more realistic by avoiding black or very dark tiles. Instead, use tiles that are a darker tone of the background colour, or experiment with colours for the shadow that contain a hint of the complementary colour of the object. For example, with a red shape try using a dark green for the shadow.

Drop shadows are very effective with lettering, making the words of a sign appear to stand out three-dimensionally from the surface. However, creating drop shadows of individual letters can be very painstaking, particularly at a small scale – work large, and create your shadows by tracing the outline of the letters first onto

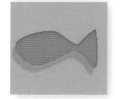

CREATING A DROP SHADOW
The graphic sequence on the left shows how simple it is to create a drop shadow. Outline the shape you want to shadow, move the outline down and to one side, then "fill" the gap in between with a shadow colour.

the baseboard then transferring the letter a second time at a set distance downwards and to the side. Make sure you keep the "offset" of the shadow outline the same for every letter. To avoid confusion, it is worth colouring in the letters and their shadows in different colours on your baseboard to guide you as you tile.

LETTERS AND NUMBERS

Drop shadows are a good way to improve the impact of letters and numbers by isolating them from the surrounding background.

ADD DEPTH

This design uses a simple drop shadow to give depth to the pond in which the Koi carp is swimming. The shadow has been created with a simple "shift" of the outline of the fish. The same outline has then been flipped over to make two more shadows which suggest that other members of the school are lurking just outside the frame of the picture.

Choosing colour palettes

Your choice of colour scheme will be dictated by the subject matter and the place where the mosaic is to be. The surroundings are especially important, you might want the mosaic to provide a dramatic colour note in an otherwise neutral room, or to echo and pick up the colours already present in the room. The main choice is between a harmonious scheme, which will create a quiet, gentle effect, and a contrasting, eye-catching one, making use of primary and complementary colours.

COLOUR PALETTE: BLACK AND GREY

You could make an exciting mosaic using nothing but a range of blacks and greys, relying on contrasts of tone to create excitement. But blacks and greys are also an excellent foil for both subtle and vivid colours, as shown below and opposite.

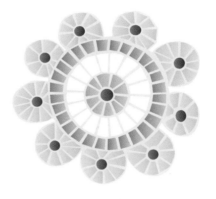

SIMPLE BLACK AND GREY PALETTE

Dark grey

Mid grey

White

PASTELS

Light grey

Baby pink

Baby blue

Dark grey

Mid grey

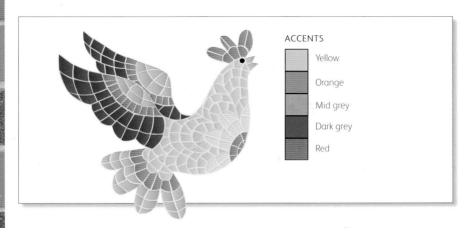

ACCENTS

- Yellow
- Orange
- Mid grey
- Dark grey
- Red

COMPLEMENTARY

- Blue grey
- Orange grey
- Mid grey
- White

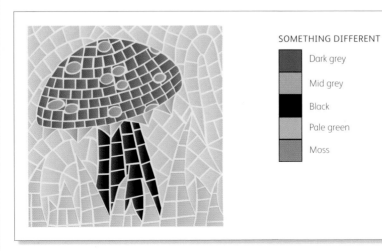

SOMETHING DIFFERENT

- Dark grey
- Mid grey
- Black
- Pale green
- Moss

COLOUR PALETTE: BLUES

As a group, the blues are cool, recessive colours, which tend to go back in space when combined with hot colours like reds and oranges. But a harmonious colour scheme of nothing but blues and perhaps some purples has distinct possibilities, as there is a very wide tonal range in this group of colours. For a more dynamic effect, try pairing blue with its complementary colour, orange.

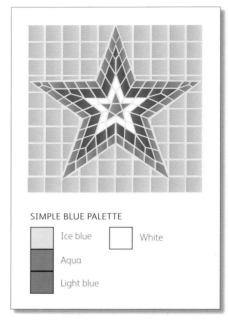

SIMPLE BLUE PALETTE

- Ice blue
- White
- Aqua
- Light blue

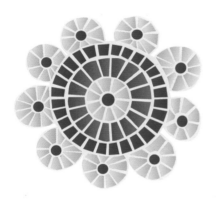

SIMPLE BLUE PALETTE

- Dark blue
- Royal blue
- Ice blue

PASTELS

- Ice blue
- Pale lemon
- Lilac
- Aqua

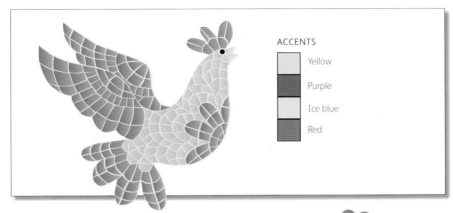

ACCENTS

Yellow

Purple

Ice blue

Red

COMPLEMENTARY

Orange

Peach

Light blue

Ice blue

SOMETHING DIFFERENT

Teal

Ice blue

Royal blue

Dark orange

Grey

COLOUR PALETTE: PURPLES

Purples can be slightly overpowering if
used at full strength, as they are typically
deep in tone, but the colour group includes
a range of paler mauves and mauve-greys,
which can be combined effectively with
many other colours. The butterfly (bottom)
shows the use of a gentle, harmonious
colour scheme, while the cockerel (top
opposite) exploits the purple-yellow
complementary contrast.

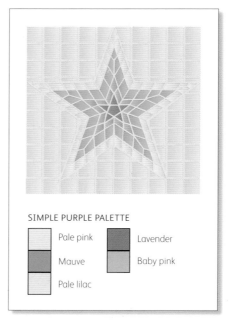

SIMPLE PURPLE PALETTE

Pale pink · Lavender
Mauve · Baby pink
Pale lilac

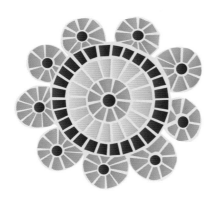

SIMPLE PURPLE PALETTE

Dark purple
Purple
Lilac

PASTELS

Pale pink
Pale purple
Pale lavender
Ice blue
Dark lilac

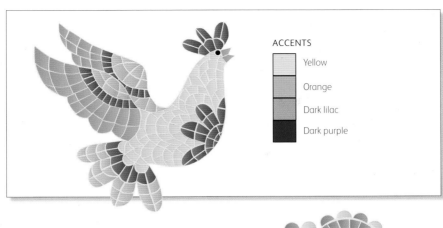

ACCENTS

Yellow

Orange

Dark lilac

Dark purple

COMPLEMENTARY

Bright yellow

Pale yellow

Dark lilac

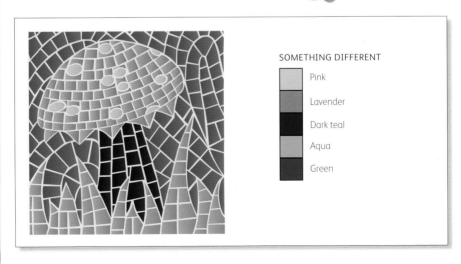

SOMETHING DIFFERENT

Pink

Lavender

Dark teal

Aqua

Green

COLOUR PALETTE: REDS

Red is known as a hot colour, one that advances in space and catches the eye, which is why it is universally used – at full strength – for warning signs. But harmonious colour schemes can be created by combining the paler shades of red with pinks, yellows and other colours of the same "family". For more drama, juxtapose fully saturated red with equally strong green, its complementary colour.

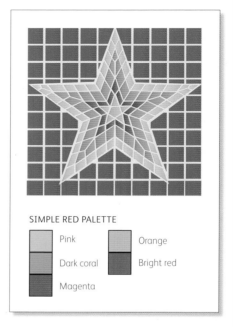

SIMPLE RED PALETTE

Pink		Orange	
Dark coral		Bright red	
Magenta			

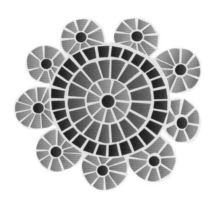

SIMPLE RED PALETTE

- Bright red
- Rust
- Brown

PASTELS

- Pale yellow
- Pale peach
- Peach
- Pale pink

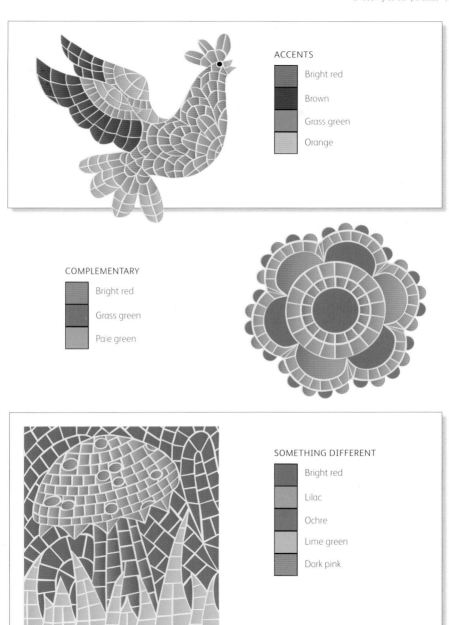

ACCENTS

Bright red

Brown

Grass green

Orange

COMPLEMENTARY

Bright red

Grass green

Pale green

SOMETHING DIFFERENT

Bright red

Lilac

Ochre

Lime green

Dark pink

COLOUR PALETTE: ORANGES

Orange is a vivid secondary colour, a mixture of red and yellow and is lighter in tone than a full-strength red. It could be used with deep reds to provide tonal contrast. As the butterfly example shows, a harmonious colour scheme can be achieved by using muted orange with yellows, mauves and touches of deep red. Orange is at it most vibrant, however, when paired with its complementary, blue.

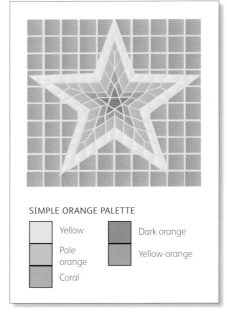

SIMPLE ORANGE PALETTE

▢	Yellow	▨	Dark orange
▨	Pale orange	▨	Yellow-orange
▨	Coral		

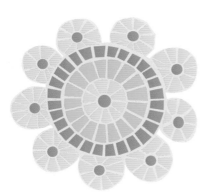

SIMPLE ORANGE PALETTE

▨	Yellow-orange
▨	Pale yellow-orange
▢	Palest yellow-orange

PASTELS

▨	Pale coral
▢	Pale yellow
▨	Pale yellow-orange
▢	Pale pink
▢	Pale lilac

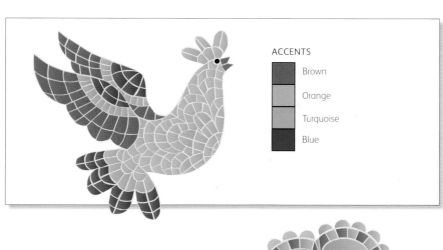

ACCENTS

- Brown
- Orange
- Turquoise
- Blue

COMPLEMENTARY

- Orange
- Pale orange
- Light blue
- Blue

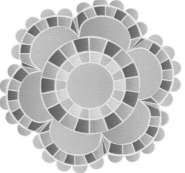

SOMETHING DIFFERENT

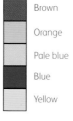

- Brown
- Orange
- Pale blue
- Blue
- Yellow

COLOUR PALETTE: YELLOWS

The yellow colour group has a smaller tonal range than any of the others; all yellows are relatively pale. It will thus need tonal contrast to be brought in by other colours, of which there is a wide choice. Yellow looks lovely against blacks and greys, and makes a good background for richer-toned hues. For vibrant contrast it can be paired with its complementary, purple.

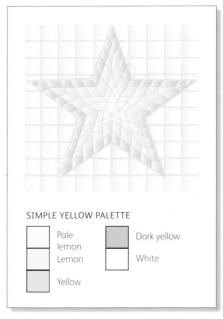

SIMPLE YELLOW PALETTE

	Pale lemon		Dark yellow
	Lemon		White
	Yellow		

SIMPLE YELLOW PALETTE

	Lemon
	Yellow
	Dark yellow

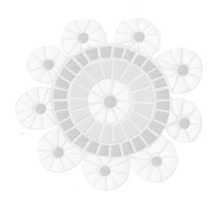

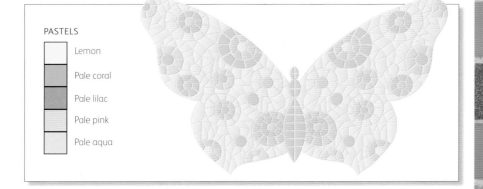

PASTELS

	Lemon
	Pale coral
	Pale lilac
	Pale pink
	Pale aqua

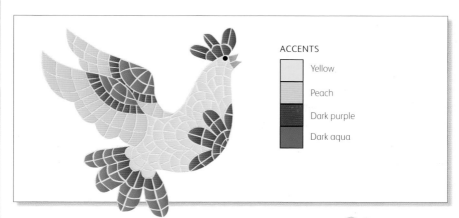

ACCENTS

- Yellow
- Peach
- Dark purple
- Dark aqua

COMPLEMENTARY

- Orange
- Yellow
- Purple

SOMETHING DIFFERENT

- Pink
- Yellow
- Peach
- Dark blue
- Cream

COLOUR PALETTE: GREENS

Like blue, green is a cool, recessive colour, with equally wide variations of tone and colour, ranging from near-blacks to the lightest whispers of bluish or yellowish green. For harmonious effects, use greens with yellows, blues and similarly toned pinks, while for dramatic contrast juxtapose a strong, relatively warm green with its complementary, red.

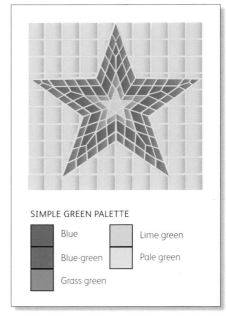

SIMPLE GREEN PALETTE

Blue		Lime green	
Blue-green		Pale green	
Grass green			

SIMPLE GREEN PALETTE

Dark green

Grass green

Pale green

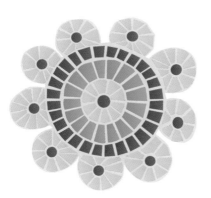

PASTELS

Pale yellow

Pale grey-green

Pale aqua

Pale blue

Pale pink

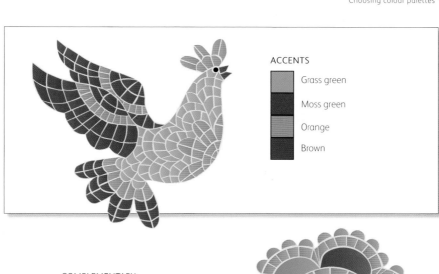

ACCENTS

Grass green

Moss green

Orange

Brown

COMPLEMENTARY

Grass green

Dark green

Bright red

SOMETHING DIFFERENT

Grass green

Dark blue

Orange

Yellow

Pale aqua

COLOUR PALETTE: BROWNS

Brown is often thought of as a dull and uniform colour, but there are countless different hues and shades of brown, any of which can be used to advantage in a colour palette. As with the blacks and greys (see page 150), you could make a monochromatic mosaic relying on tonal contrast with browns alone, or you can use them as a foil for brighter colours, as suggested in the cockerel image opposite.

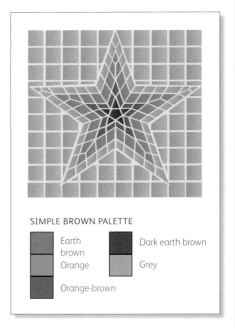

SIMPLE BROWN PALETTE

	Earth brown		Dark earth brown
	Orange		Grey
	Orange-brown		

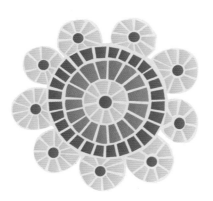

SIMPLE BROWN PALETTE

	Brown
	Deep pink
	Rose pink

PASTELS

	Light green
	Cream
	Terra cotta
	Peach
	Grey

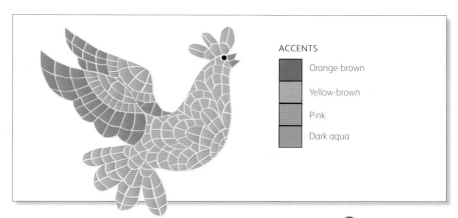

ACCENTS

- Orange-brown
- Yellow-brown
- Pink
- Dark aqua

COMPLEMENTARY

- Dark brown
- Beige
- Rose pink

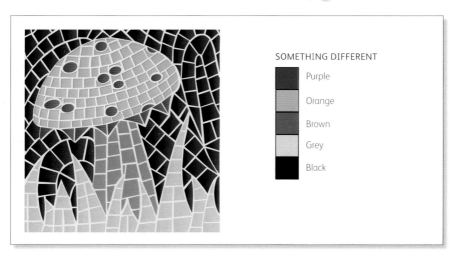

SOMETHING DIFFERENT

- Purple
- Orange
- Brown
- Grey
- Black

6 Transfer techniques

Often the location a mosaic is to be placed in, or the materials that are utlilized will require the mosaic to be physically transferred from one location to another. This chapter looks at all the different ways that a temporary support can be used to hold together tiles so that a piece can be easily installed wherever you want it.

The direct method: mesh

Mosaic tile mesh is a net of flexible plastic material. Once your tiles are glued to the mesh it acts as a temporary support so that you can move the piece to its permanent site and set it in adhesive. The big advantage of mesh is that you are working the "right" way around, so you can see what you are doing.

Tools

Pen
Ruler
Paintbrush or spatula
Craft knife or scissors
Mallet or hammer

Materials

Paper
Baking parchment or silicone-backed paper
Masking tape
Mosaic tile mesh
Tiles
White craft glue
Grout

1 Laying down the drawing
Prepare your design on paper and lay the finished drawing on your work surface.

2 Laying down a backing sheet
On your worktop, tape down a glue-resistant sheet of paper such as baking parchment or silicone-backed paper. This is vital to ensure that you can lift off the mesh and tiles when they are dry and they do not become permanently attached to your table. The sheet should be comfortably wider and taller than the design – say 50 mm (2 in) bigger all around.

Mosaic tile mesh can be used as a temporary support for a mosaic.

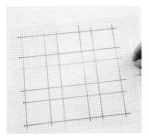  

3 Cutting the mesh
Mosaic tile mesh is available from specialist suppliers in pre-cut squares or as lengths cut from a roll. If the finished piece is large, tile it in convenient sections which you can then piece together on-site. Avoid working on an area bigger than 300 x 300 mm (12 x 12 in) or you will find the sheets of mesh heavy and unmanageable when covered with tiles. Allow a border of at least 10 mm (⅜ in) of mesh larger around each section, and tape this down.

4 Tiling
Proceed with laying the tiles exactly as if working in the direct method onto a board (see page 80). Glue a small area at a time, making sure to cover the strands of mesh, and place your tiles. Don't overdo the glue – if you fill in the "cells" of the mesh this will form a barrier preventing the back of the tiles from adhering in their final location. Allow the glue to dry thoroughly – be patient and don't move the tiles or you risk dislodging them from the mesh.

5 Removing the tiles
With a craft knife or scissors, cut through the tape holding the mesh and backing sheet to the work surface and cut off all remnants of mesh as close to the edge of the tiles as possible. Carefully peel off and discard the "release sheet".

6 Mounting the mosaic
Carry the mesh and tile sheets to the site – support them on a board if necessary. Spread a generous layer of glue to match the area of the first sheet and press the mesh backing firmly into it. Use a small piece of board and a mallet or hammer to tap over the surface of the tiles to ensure they are level. Now lay the next sheet, taking care to line up the design. When all the sheets are laid, leave them to dry. (On a vertical surface, use tape to support each section while it sets.) Finally, grout and clean.

The indirect method: paper

The paper method is a traditional way of creating a mosaic "off-site". The mosaic is laid the "wrong" way around – with the surface of the tiles that will be finally displayed facing downwards and the tile backs facing towards you. It is not until the very end of the process that you will see the front face of the tiles or the design the "right" way around.

Tools

Pen

Scissors

Paintbrush or spatula

Tray or board

Sponge

Materials

Brown parcel paper

Water-soluble glue (craft glue, wallpaper paste, or flour paste)

White craft glue

Grout

1 Cutting the transfer paper
Use brown parcel paper for this method – it is strong and stable and, most importantly, will soak up water when you want to remove it from the tiles at the end. Cut a sheet to accommodate your design comfortably. If you are working on a large design break it down into sections no larger than 300 x 300 mm (12 x 12 in) so that the sheets will be manageable when covered in tiles.

2 Transferring your design
Transfer your drawing onto the brown paper. Remember that the end result will be back to front – make sure that letters and numbers are the correct way around. If you have access to a lightbox (you can improvize using a window, see page 116) you can flip the design by tracing over the back of the sheet and using this as the "original" that you transfer.
Go over the transferred design with a permanent marker so that you can see it clearly.

3 Mixing the glue
Before spreading any glue onto the paper, check that it is water-soluble – you can use craft glue, wallpaper paste or even a simple flour paste. Do not use the same white glue that you would use for direct tiling.

4 Laying the tiles

Start laying the tiles – remembering to place them upside-down – pressing the "right" side of the tile into the glue. Complete laying the mosaic as normal, working on a small area at a time and then allowing it to dry.

5 Gluing the tiles

Move the finished sheets to the site. Put them on a tray or boards to support them – old pizza boxes are ideal for single sheets and you can stack several on top of each other. Next, glue an area of the mounting surface with a good layer of waterproof adhesive extending over an area slightly larger than the first sheet you want to lay. Flip the sheet over, and lay the back surface of the tiles carefully onto the glue. Check and adjust the position then press the sheet down more firmly using a rubber squeegee or roller. Complete all the sections, aligning them carefully. Allow the glue to dry thoroughly.

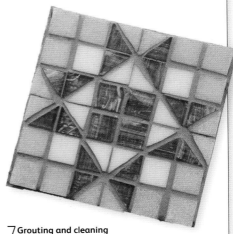

6 Soaking away the backing

Use a wet sponge to soak the brown paper thoroughly. Leave the water to sink in and then give it a second soaking. Allow the water to soak into the paper for fifteen minutes, splashing on more if necessary. Eventually, the paper should loosen and, if you are lucky, you should be able to peel the brown paper off in one gentle movement. Work carefully; you may need to re-stick any loose tiles as you go.

7 Grouting and cleaning

After removing the paper, clean off the surface of the mosaic and allow it to dry before grouting in the usual way.

The double indirect method

The double indirect method is an extension of the indirect method (see page 170) which allows you to lay out a design the "right" way around, and uses two transfer steps to install the finished piece in situ. This allows you to work with materials where the back of different tile pieces is always the same – for example, household ceramic tiles which have an earthenware base – so that you cannot see the colour or pattern which is on the glazed surface.

Materials
Brown parcel paper
Ceramic tiles
Water-soluble craft glue
PVA
MDF
Waterproof glue or tile adhesive
Grout

Tools
Pen or pencil
Ruler
Scissors
Paintbrush
Book or block of wood
Sponge

1 **Draw on the first transfer sheet**
Draw or trace your design onto a first sheet of brown paper.

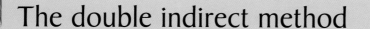

TIP:

Be warned – this method requires great care and patience. In summary, you lay and glue your mosaic directly onto a first sheet of temporary transfer paper, then glue the surface of the completed design onto a second transfer sheet, before removing the first sheet and gluing the exposed back of the tiles into their final location.

2 Lay your tiles

The procedure at this stage is fairly simple – work exactly as if following the direct method (see page 80). Glue your tile pieces directly over the design on the paper backing – making sure, however, that you use a weak mix of water-soluble craft glue to provide the temporary adhesion for this first step. Take extra care to make sure everything is positioned absolutely accurately; any sloppiness will be magnified by the additional transfer step in this method.

3 Let the "direct sheet" dry

Leave the tiles to dry on the sheet of brown paper, then trim away any excess backing. Now take a slightly larger second sheet of brown paper and apply a generous coating of glue – again it must be water-soluble, but using a slightly stronger mix. Now turn over the piece and carefully lay it with the tile surface face down onto the wet adhesive.

4 Weight down the tiles

Use a book or a block of wood to firmly press the surface of the tiles into the glue on the second transfer sheet, and leave to dry thoroughly.

5 Soak the first sheet

When the second application of glue is thoroughly dry, remove any weights, and then soak off the first backing sheet using a sponge and warm water. Work carefully – don't swamp the piece with water otherwise you risk not only dissolving the glue on the first transfer sheet, but also releasing the glue on the sheet below.

6 Peel off the first sheet

As the water takes effect on the glue, carefully peel away the first sheet of brown paper. Be gentle, so as not to loosen the tiles from the second sheet – dab at any stubborn areas with the sponge, and wait a bit longer for the glue to loosen. When all the paper is removed, you should be left looking at the backs of the tile pieces, with the front surface of the design still securely glued, face down, to the second sheet of paper.

7 Trim away excess backing

Tidy up the second transfer sheet by trimming away any excess that extends beyond the outline of the tiles.

8 Prepare the final surface

Lay a generous amount of adhesive onto the surface where the piece is to be finally sited – this time you need to use an appropriate permanent waterproof glue or tile adhesive.

9 Lay the tiles

Now lay the exposed backs of the tiles into the glue with the second transfer sheet of paper facing towards you – work over the surface of the mosaic with a block of wood and a mallet, tapping lightly to ensure that every tile piece is pressed firmly into the adhesive. Again, use a weighted board to keep the tiles in place while the adhesive sets.

10 Remove the second transfer sheet
Let the adhesive set completely over a couple of days (transfer sheets slow the drying time of most adhesives quite considerably). Then soak the surface of the brown paper thoroughly with warm water to finally reveal the finished design.

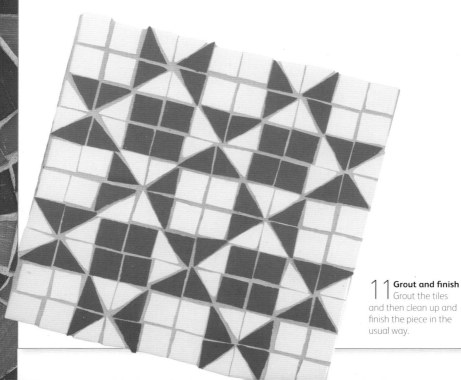

11 Grout and finish
Grout the tiles and then clean up and finish the piece in the usual way.

7 Grouting and finishing

Grout provides the finishing touch to a mosaic, visually "holding" the design together. Successful grouting is about more than understanding how to mix and apply different types of grout – the colour and tone of grout you choose is perhaps even more important. This chapter also shows you how to clean the finished piece and the different techniques you can use to mount and display your work.

Mixing and colouring grouts

Grouts come in different types but ready-mixed grout is perhaps the simplest to use as it requires no preparation or careful measurement of quantities. You can mix in pigment to colour the grout to suit your design.

Tools

Plastic bowl with a sealable lid
Spoon or spatula
Rubber gloves
Measuring jug
Pail or basin

Materials

Ready-mixed or powdered grout
Acrylic paint or poster paint

PREPARING READY-MIXED GROUTS

Ready-mixed grout is readily available from hardware shops and is supplied in resealable tubs which, if used correctly, allow you to use the grout for several weeks after it has first been opened. Ready-mixed grout is not generally suitable for outdoor use (see "Preparing waterproof grouts for outside", page 183).

1 Transferring the grout to a container

Work with just the amount of grout you will need to complete a piece — otherwise your main stock of grout will dry out and deteriorate. Begin by transferring a generous amount into a strong plastic mixing bowl. Old ice-cream containers are ideal for mixing grout as they are strong and disposable, and have a sealable lid.

2 Using white grout

Ready-mixed grout is most often coloured white. You will quickly learn that grout used "straight from the tub" can have an overpowering effect, creating a grid of bright tramlines over your design which fragments the overall effect, as in the mosaic letter E, below. Ready-mixed grouts are sometimes available in a neutral grey or a small range of brighter colours. However, these are expensive, and usually it is better to add colour yourself to achieve the shade you need.

3 Mixing in pigment

Liquid acrylic paint – which is water-based – is the best type of colourant to use with ready-mixed grout. You can also used ready-mixed or powdered "poster" paints. Because the grout already contains white pigment, any colour you add will be weakened to a pastel shade; to make a dark tone or strong colour you will need to add quite a lot of paint.

4 Stirring in the pigment

Mix the pigment into the grout thoroughly with a spoon or spatula otherwise the effect may be uneven when you grout your piece. Grouting is an irreversible process so take time to mix the grout properly and avoid problems later. Make sure you mix enough grout – it is very difficult to make a second, matching batch if you run out.

KEEP CONTAINERS SEALED

Until you actually need your grout – as well as after you have applied it – make sure you tightly reseal all containers to prevent the grout from drying out and becoming unworkable.

SEE ALSO

Grouts, page 40

Tools and equipment, page 42

PREPARING POWDERED GROUTS

Powdered grouts are usually cement-powder based and are designed to be mixed as and when required. Read the instructions on the packaging to make sure you get the ratio of powder to water right. Measure properly and don't guess, otherwise you risk making a horrible sloppy mess that will run everywhere and fail to set. Rubber gloves are essential – cement powders can irritate the skin.

1 Putting the powder in a bowl
Always add liquid to the cement powder, not the other way around. If you want to colour your grout (see page 184), it is best done while the grout is in a dry state by adding a powder pigment.

2 Adding the water
Pile the grout into a little mound, and make a depression in the top so it looks like a mini volcano. Use a measuring jug to pour the water, a little at a time, into the "crater". Gradually stir in grout from the sides of the crater, then remake the crater and add more water.

3 Judging when to stop
As the grout approaches the correct consistency, add water more cautiously. The grout should be moist and not gritty in appearance, but stiff enough to keep its shape when you stir it with a spatula. When you judge that it is ready, cover it with clingwrap or a damp cloth until you are ready to use it – don't delay longer than necessary.

PREPARING WATERPROOF GROUTS FOR OUTSIDE

Sturdy equipment is required for working with cement-based, external-use grouts. A strong builder's pail is ideal and gloves are essential as this type of grout has a high lime content, which can irritate the skin. If you don't have an outdoor tap, then fill up plenty of containers with water and take them outside before you start mixing the grout so that no mess is carried back inside on your shoes.

1 Select the correct grout

If you are grouting mosaics for use in a wet room or in an outdoor environment, make absolutely sure that you obtain the correct product for external use. All grouts are waterproof to some extent, but a grout that is going to be submerged in water, and subject to extremely low or freezing temperatures is a specialist product.

2 Work quickly

Waterproof grouts are made to "set-up" within a set time of being mixed, so once you have started to add water to them you need to work quickly. Follow the instructions to achieve the correct consistency, mixing only enough as you can use within the working time specified.

3 Discard excess grout

Once the chemical reaction is underway within a waterproof grout there is little you can do to slow it, although the manufacturer may supply specialist retardants to lengthen the setting time. Using the grout in cooler/humid conditions may also slow it down. If a batch of grout begins to dry out too soon you have no choice but to throw it away. Thoroughly clean out your mixing container (any residue may act as a catalyst, accelerating the drying time of the next batch) and mix a smaller, more manageable quantity of fresh grout.

THE EFFECTS OF DIFFERENT COLOURED GROUTS

Having spent hours completing your mosaic, it is important to get the grout colour exactly right. Below you can see how the choice of grout can completely alter the impact produced by an identical use of colours and arrangement of tiles.

WHITE GROUT

In this sample, a plain white grout was used. The high contrast of the grout with the colours of the surrounding tiles tends to fragment the design. Sometimes that effect may be desirable, but generally white grout overpowers the tiles and is best avoided. (Bear in mind too that white grout tends to discolour over time and stains easily.)

GREY GROUT

A light to mid grey is often the safest grout colour to choose – grey appears neutral when combined with most colours, while tonally it tends to form a bridge between tiles rather than a separator.

 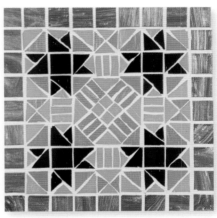

BLACK/DARK GREY GROUT

This is perhaps one of the most effective grout choices on these pages. It gives the tiles a strong emphasis – rather like the leading in a stained glass window. The orange and red tiles are given particular definition and sharpness by the dark tone of the grout. But again, it is a choice that works well on this particular colour mix – on lighter, pastel shades this grout choice would probably prove overwhelming.

ORANGE GROUT

Here a coloured grout has been used, chosen to complement the colour palette of the piece. The choice of a brightly coloured grout with equally bright tiles does not always have the expected effect. In this case, the grout seems to detract from the brightness of the orange and red tiles, compared to other grout choices on these pages that seem to emphasize the colours.

Applying grout

Be patient – make sure that the tiles are firmly in place and the glue has dried thoroughly before starting to grout. White craft glues are water-based, and unless they have completely hardened they will soften under the action of the grouting and tile pieces may dislodge.

Tools
Spoon
Rubber gloves
Rubber grouting squeegee
Sponge
Airtight container or clingwrap
Cloth

Materials
Ungrouted mosaic
Grout

1 Starting to grout
Spoon a small mound of freshly mixed grout onto an area of the mosaic. Use a rubber grouting squeegee to press the grout into the gaps between the tiles. Concentrate at first on downward pressure to fill the gaps to their bases – don't just slide the squeegee over the surface or you will create a skin that does not grip and support the tile pieces, and will crack as the grout dries.

2 Adding more grout
Depending on the width and depth of your grout lines, even a small mosaic can absorb a large amount of grout. At this stage you want there to be excess grout on the surface of the tiles which you keep pressing downwards.

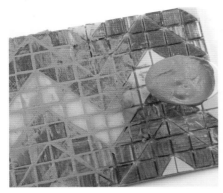

3 Moving onto the next area
Repeat the process for the next part of the mosaic. Again, concentrate on a manageable area, pressing the squeegee more downwards than across the surface.

4 Scraping off the excess
When you are satisfied that the gaps between the tiles can absorb no more grout, use your squeegee or a scraper to lift off the excess. Discard this grout – don't add it back to your stock of grout to reuse – it will spoil fresh grout. Reseal any grout that you have not used with clingwrap or an airtight lid.

5 Wiping off excess grout
Leave the grout for around half an hour, then check with your finger that it has largely set. With a lightly dampened cloth wipe over the surface of the mosaic to clean off the worst deposits of grout. Use a polishing action with a flat pad of cloth – avoid digging into the gaps. Don't over-soak the cloth as this will also disturb the grout. You will find a light film of grout still remains – you can polish this off when the piece has completely dried. Leave the piece for at least 24 hours to be sure the grout is completely dry.

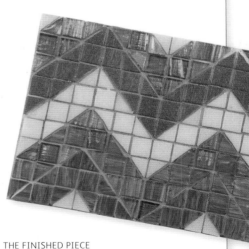

THE FINISHED PIECE
It is the grout that transforms the separate pieces of tile into a unified design, so always take the time to grout with care.

Making a slab

One of the easiest ways to make a mosaic which is suitable for siting outdoors is to cast a paving slab with a mosaic surface. This has the advantage of allowing you to make up slabs inside rather than out of doors, where you are at the mercy of the weather. You can make up a number of mosaic paving slabs and intermingle them with plain slabs of the same size to provide interest to a paved area. Alternatively, sink the finished slabs into a lawn to make a stepping-stone path.

MAKING A MOSAIC SLAB

The slab is made up within a wooden frame. This technique is similar to the indirect method (see page 170) in that you work by laying your mosaic face-down into the frame, then casting the slab onto the back of the tiles. Therefore you do not see the finished mosaic until the very end when the frame is taken apart and removed.

1 Making a frame

You can buy a casting frame from a specialist supplier or make one yourself. The frame is a wooden board cut from a piece of MDF or marine ply, on which sits a wooden "wall" of wood the thickness of the slab – around 50 mm (2 in) high and 25 mm (1 in) thick. The wall is held firmly to the base by screws or bolts. If you make your own frame to a specific size, to match existing paving slabs for example, remember that the size of the finished slab will be the same as the inside measurement of your frame.

Materials

Wooden casting frame
Brown paper
Tiles suitable for use outdoors
Water-soluble glue
Petroleum jelly
Cement
Water
Sharp sand
Chicken wire

Tools

Paintbrush
Rubber gloves
Squeegee
Trowel
Piece of wood longer than the casting frame
Damp sacking or plastic
Sponge

2 **Follow the instructions for the indirect method**
Cut a piece of brown paper slightly smaller than the internal measurement of your frame, then transfer your design to the paper (see page 128). It is easier to work on the mosaic outside of the frame and then transfer it back into the frame when it is complete. Stick the pieces face-down onto the paper using a weak, water-soluble glue. In this example, marble tiles that are tolerant of freezing temperatures were used.

3 **Preparing the frame**
Smear a generous amount of petroleum jelly over the inside of the made-up frame – this acts as a release agent so that the slab does not get damaged through the cement binding too tightly to the frame. Place the finished design face (paper) side down onto the base. Make a final check, adjusting any badly spaced tiles and re-gluing loose ones.

4 **Pre-grouting**
Some people like to pre-grout the mosaic at this stage. This fills the gaps between the tiles which may make them less likely to move when you add the bulk of cement for the slab. If you do pre-grout, use a mixture of cement and water. Allow this grout to "set-up".

5 Mixing the cement

Use a "strong" cement mix: three parts sharp sand to one part cement. Add only enough water to make the cement workable – it should feel on the dry side. Use a trowel to fill the frame halfway up the walls, pressing the cement firmly into the angles of the frame so that it is nice and dense.

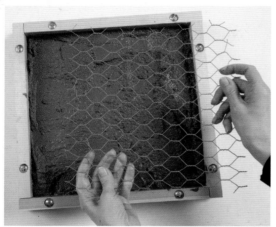

6 Adding reinforcement

Lay a piece of chicken wire on top of the cement layer – it should be 25 mm (1 in) smaller all around so that it does not protrude from the sides of the finished slab.

7 Continue adding cement

Press the wire flat, then continue adding cement up to the top of the frame. The chicken wire will reinforce the cement, making it stronger when you move and install the slab. Level off the back of the slab with a piece of wood slightly longer than the width of the frame. Smooth the surface by flicking water onto it with an old paintbrush and polishing it in a circular action with a metal trowel.

8 Removing the frame

Cover the back of the slab with a piece of damp sacking or plastic – this is to slow the drying out of the slab and make it stronger. Leave the slab for at least a week so that the cement thoroughly goes off. Undo the screws holding the frame together and gently pry it apart. Soak the surface of the brown paper which is revealed when you remove the baseboard, and carefully peel the backing away to – at last! – reveal the surface of the tiles.

9 Re-grouting

Go over the front of the mosaic again with a thinner mix of just cement and water. Let this nearly "set-up". then clean up with a damp sponge. Rewrap and leave to dry out further for at least another week before installing in your patio or garden.

Polishing and finishing

There are several techniques you can use to remove small blemishes from your completed mosaics and make the finished pieces really sparkle and shine.

Materials
Grout
Glass polish

Tools
Sponge
Pan scourer
Toothpick
Buffing cloth

1 **Remove grout residue**
A couple of hours after grouting a mosaic, you will find that there is a light scum of grout over the entire surface of the tiles that noticeably dulls the tile colours. Generously soak a light-gauge sponge, then rub over the surface of the mosaic. Rinse the sponge and repeat several times, changing the water you use frequently, until all of the residue is removed.

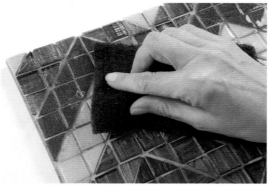

2 **Scour off glue spots**
It is quite common, if you are using PVA glue to stick down your mosaics, for small deposits to end up on the surface of the tiles. Because of the translucency of the glue when dry, you often won't notice glue residue until the final clean-up. Provided that the grout has completely set, you can attack any small deposits of glue with something quite abrasive such as a pan scourer.

3 Use a stick on larger glue spots

Thicker deposits of glue can be removed by poking and scraping with a toothpick or similar-sized piece of wood (avoid using metal tools which may scratch or discolour the glazed surface of the tiles).

4 Repair any grout "holes"

Mix up a small amount of matching grout and use this to repair any holes in the grout lines. Again, you can use a wooden toothpick or similar to press the grout into any holes then, when dry, carefully clean up and polish around the repaired areas.

5 Shine the finished piece

A last optional step is to use a proprietary glass polish across the surface of the mosaic, and then bring this to a shine with a buffing cloth. However, some designs might not suit this approach, and you may want to leave the tiles with a more natural, subdued finish.

Cleaning up and polishing your mosaic adds the finishing touch.

Mounting

If you are making a mosaic on a baseboard it is worth planning in advance how you will finally mount it to the wall. Finished mosaics can be quite heavy when you add together the weight of a wooden backing, a large area of tiles, and a good volume of grout. Any mountings you use should be fairly substantial. It is also a good idea to make your screw holes or attach any embedded hanging plates before you begin tiling as adding them afterward risks damaging your work.

Materials

Mirror plates
Screws
Wall plugs
Keyhole plates

Tools

Screwdriver
Pencil
Spirit level
Drill
Masonry drill bit
Large drill bit
Craft knife
Countersink drill bit

FITTING MIRROR PLATES

Mirror plates are metal fittings, usually made of brass, that are screwed to the back of the baseboard with two shallow screws. When viewed from the front, the third hole of the fitting protrudes beyond the perimeter of the base board so that it can be screwed into the surrounding wall.

1 Marking up the drill points

After screwing the mirror plates to the piece, hold it up to the wall in the position you want it and mark where the holes will need to be drilled for the mounting screws.

2 Checking the level
Use a spirit level to make sure the drill holes are correctly aligned so that the piece will be straight.

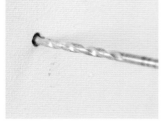

3 Drilling the holes
For mounting on a solid masonry wall you will need to use screws combined with wall plugs. Wall plugs are colour coded in different sizes – make sure you select a plug and screw combination suitable for the mirror plate. Drill the correct size hole using a masonry bit of the diameter recommended by the plug manufacturer.

4 Be safe!
Take care not to drill through any concealed wires or pipes (if in doubt buy a special tester from a DIY store which can alert you to the presence of hidden metalwork or electrical currents).

5 Screwing to the wall
When everything is ready, ask someone to hold up the piece while you screw it firmly to the wall. You can paint over the mirror plate and screw with paint that matches the wall to conceal the fittings if you want.

SLOTTED OR KEYHOLE PLATES

Slotted or keyhole plates are similar to ordinary mirror plates, but have
a special slot that can be slipped over the screw once it is in the wall. They
are particularly useful if you need to hang something by yourself, as you do
not have to support the weight of the piece while you place the screws in the wall.

MAKING A CONCEALED KEYHOLE MOUNT

You can use keyhole plates on the back of your piece to hide the fitting completely.

1 Positioning the plate
Centre and draw around the
plate with a pencil to show the
position of the screws and keyhole.

2 Making the slot
Use a large-diameter drill bit to
make two or three holes to create
a long slot behind the keyhole.

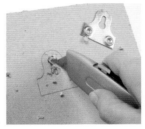

3 Neatening the slot
Neaten the slot with a chisel
or craft knife so that the sides are
straight and neat. Take care not to
drill through the back of the board
and damage the mosaic.

4 Fixing the keyhole plate
Now drill the screw holes and
mount the plate over the slot.
Check that you can insert and
remove a round-headed screw but
that the keyhole slot fits snugly
over the screwhead.

5 Hanging the piece
Drill your hole in the wall. Insert
a wall plug, then screw in the
round-headed screw – leaving
it standing out 12.5 mm (½ in)
from the wall surface. Now you
should be able to hang the piece
by sliding the screwhead into the
keyhole plate on the back of the
piece so that it sits firmly in place.

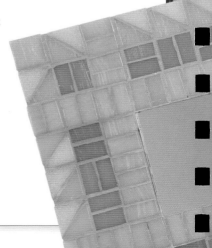

MAKING CONCEALED CORNER MOUNTS

This is one of the simplest ways to neatly and safely mount mosaic pieces to the wall, while concealing the fittings. However, it is very permanent as "demounting" the piece will mean damaging the surface of the mosaic to remove the hidden fittings.

1 Drilling the screwholes
Before drawing up your design on the baseboard, drill holes in each corner, positioning them so that they will be underneath a whole tile if possible.

2 Countersinking the screwholes
Use a countersink bit to bevel the hole so that the screwhead will be completely flush with the surface of the baseboard.

3 Concealing the fittings
Complete your mosaic, but leave the corner holes exposed. Use a pencil to mark up the position of the four corner holes on the wall, then drill and plug the holes. Hold up the mosaic (you will probably need someone else to help you) and screw it firmly to the wall. Place and glue the missing tiles over the screwheads and, when dry, grout the added tiles in place.

8 Projects

The projects in this chapter have been designed to offer a range of challenges to the mosaicist. They vary in difficulty, from pieces suitable for beginners to quite complex designs that are intended for the experienced mosaicist. Each project is broken down into a series of steps, which are clearly illustrated and explained.

Project 1 : Gingham coasters

These coasters for cups and glasses use different tones of the same colours, mixed with white, to produce the effect of gingham cloth. Each coaster is tiled onto a small square of thin MDF. To make the end result more interesting and intricate, vitreous tiles were used that had been split into quarters.

Tools
Ruler
Pencil
Nippers
Fibretip pen
Paintbrush

Materials
MDF
Vitreous tiles
PVA glue
Grout
Paint
Felt
Cork pads

1 Measure and cut the baseboards
Begin by cutting out equal-sized squares of MDF. Because you will be using "quarter" vitreous tiles, each coaster needs to be a multiple of the measurement of the quarter tile plus an additional thickness for each grout line (see page 86). For the repeat of the pattern to leave "key" tiles of the same colour at each corner, the measurement of the baseboard also needs to allow for an odd number of tiles along the sides.

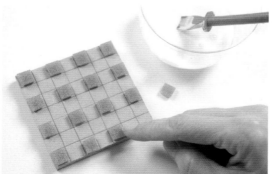

2 Start laying tiles
Prepare a stock of quarter tiles. Begin by laying the darker tiles (or whichever are the "key" tiles in the corners of the design) into your ruled-up grid.

3 Lay in a tonal sequence
Next, glue and lay all of the lighter-toned tiles, and then finish each coaster with the white pieces. (As you put more and more tiles into the grid you will realize the importance of calculating the grid to accommodate both the cut tiles and the grout line.)

4 Grout and finish
Complete the mosaic then grout and polish the tiles. To provide a neat finish, paint the edges of each coaster with a suitable matching paint, then cut a piece of felt as a backing material. Mark the felt by drawing around the baseboard with a fibretip pen, offsetting it slightly so that the felt is slightly smaller and will not protrude around the edges.

5 Glue on the felt backing
Apply PVA to the back of the board, press the felt firmly in position, and then leave it to dry. Alternatively, you could paint the back of the coasters and use cork pads.

6 Create varied sets of coasters
Starting with this very simple design, you can add interest by making the coasters up into sets of different combinations of colours. This is an example of a design where the effect of the whole piece is more effective than that of the individual pieces.

Project 2: Trivet

A trivet is a "hot-plate" that is intended to protect tabletops and work surfaces from damage by saucepans or oven dishes. A mosaic makes an ideal surface for a trivet, because ceramic material is heat-resistant and, providing the grout is sealed, easy to clean.

Tools
Pencil
Scissors
Nippers
Permanent marker
Paintbrush

Materials
Paper
Masking tape
MDF
Vitreous tiles
PVA glue
Paint
Grout

1 Create a design using cut-outs
Using the template method described on pages 62–65, make your design up as a number of paper cut-outs that you can position onto a sheet of drawing paper the same size as the board. Arrange the cut-outs to your satisfaction, then stick them down and colour them – this is your drawing for the piece.

2 Transfer the design
Use tracing paper to copy your cut-out design. Then rub the reverse of the tracing with a soft pencil or chalk, transfer your design to the MDF baseboard by drawing over the tracing. Darken the transferred lines if they are not dark enough so that you can clearly see the outlines when you are gluing the tiles down.

3 Start laying tiles

Start the laying by cutting the small circles at the centre of the flower heads. Place these onto your baseboard using PVA – it is important to establish these centres to work outwards from.

4 Foreground elements

Next, work on the design elements in the "foreground"; that is, items like the white flowers in this example that obscure other elements of the design. If possible cut the petals as a single tile piece – "nibbling" with your cutters to create neat symmetrical shapes.

5 Place the strong upright stalks

The upright stalks of the yellow flowers were made by splitting tiles in half and laying them end-to-end. Again, cut the leaves from one tile so that each leaf is a single piece.

6 Finish off the flowers

The large flowers are made up of two tones of orange, using a flowing opus that follows the outline. Complete the background foliage, filling in the spaces between the tiles you have laid. A useful technique is to hold the tiles over the area they need to fill and draw cutting guides onto each tile. In this way you can accurately complete an area without leaving uneven and unsightly grouting lines.

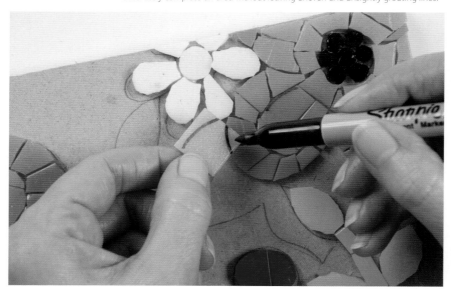

7 Complete the background

The background is best completed in a fairly irregular fashion, using small tile pieces – a more formal pattern, such as a checkerboard, is very challenging when there are lots of foreground objects to cut around so that the background tiles fit. Paint the sides of the piece in a colour to co-ordinate with the design and attach felt or cork to the reverse of the piece to prevent damage to table tops and work surfaces.

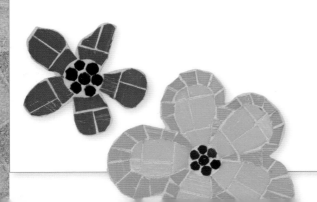

Project 3: Geometric picture

This classic geometric pattern utilizes just four tones of very similar colours. It is a strong optical piece that uses the same grid of triangular-cut tiles to create a different three-dimensional effect in each of the separate quarters of the picture.

Tools

Ruler
Pencil
Fibretip pens
Wheeled tile cutters
Paintbrush

Materials

MDF
Vitreous tiles
PVA glue
Paint
Grout

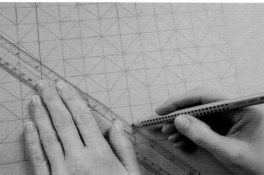

1 Mark up the board

With a rigid mathematical grid you can draw directly onto your baseboard rather than transferring the design from a separate drawing. The design consists of triangles made by splitting individual vitreous tiles across the diagonal. You must therefore make sure that the squares of the grid are large enough to allow for the split tile and the grout line in between (the squares are therefore slightly larger than the size of the uncut tile).

2 Colour in the grid

It takes extra time, but it is well worth clearly colouring in the drawing with markers. Optical designs are by their nature very visually confusing so make your mistakes now with a pen, rather than when you are gluing tiles down. Start with the darkest toned tiles to establish the repeats of each area, and then fill in each other tone in turn. Follow the patterns you can see on the finished piece or, working on a triangular grid on paper or a computer, experiment with different layouts of the tiles.

3 Pre-cut your tiles
The best way to work on this design is with everything pre-cut, so that you can concentrate on laying the pattern correctly. Cut as big a batch of tiles as you have the patience for – this example contains 800 cut tiles! Wheeled cutters are better than ordinary nippers – the wastage you would avoid on this project alone probably makes them a worthwhile investment.

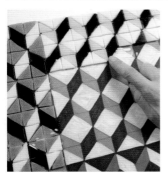

4 Work on one square at a time
You can tile the piece as you wish, but it is probably easier to work a square at a time using the pre-cut tiles of different colours as they are needed. Laying all one colour and then going back to fill in the gaps risks finding tiles squeezed out by any inaccuracies, which are then difficult to correct once the glue has set.

5 Finish and leave unframed
A mid-toned grey grout is the least intrusive choice for this example of a geometric pattern. Clean up the finished piece thoroughly, removing any grout from around the edges of the tiles and the baseboard using sandpaper. Then neatly finish the edges of the board with paint – framing this piece is not advisable, as a frame would not complement the simple grid.

TIP

Before grouting, check everything – it is surprisingly easy to lay tiles in the wrong sequence and not to notice at the time. Any mistakes discovered now can be corrected by carefully prying out the incorrectly placed tile with an old screwdriver (supported underneath by a cloth to avoid damaging surrounding tiles) and then replacing it with the correct tile. Ask someone else to double-check, and only then proceed to grouting and finishing as normal.

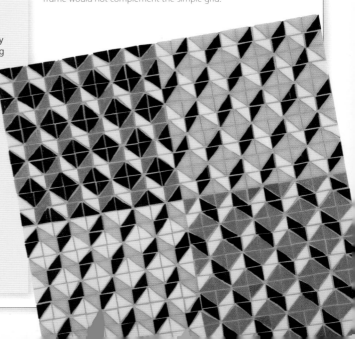

Project 4: Mirror

For this project, plain ceramic tiles were mixed with found patterned tiles that featured lots of attractive detail. It's an ideal project for using up leftovers.

Tools
Pencil
Ruler
Glue spatula
Nippers
Tabletop tile cutter

Materials
Mirror
MDF
Ceramic tiles
PVA
Grout
Masking tape

1 **Cut the baseboard**
Cut your baseboard and then draw diagonals from corner to corner to find its centre.

2 Place your mirror

A glass supplier can cut a piece of mirrored glass to the exact size you require. If you want an even border all the way around, then the piece of mirror should be the same proportion as your baseboard – if it is, then use the diagonal lines to exactly position the mirror in the centre of the board. Otherwise, use a ruler to find the vertical and horizontal centres of the mirror and place the mirror in line with centres you have established on the baseboard.

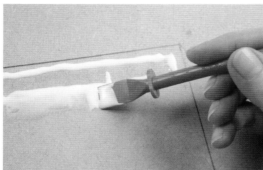

3 Glue down the mirror

Once you have centred the mirror, draw an outline in pencil, place the mirror to one side and then glue the board using PVA applied with a spatula before setting the mirror in place.

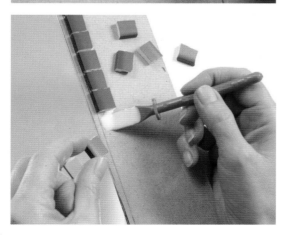

4 Tile the inner border

To give the design some definition, a plain border in a dark colour is used to outline the mirror. To give a neat inner edge, use the edges of the tiles so that there is a neat, glazed surface displayed all around the mirror. To do this, use a tabletop cutter to cut narrow strips from the edges of your tiles, then split these into short, square lengths using tile nippers.

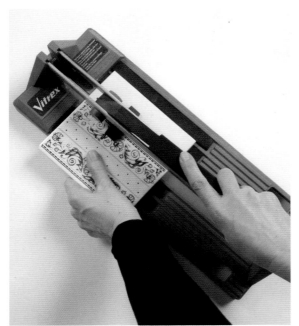

5 Cut the patterned tiles

Again, use the tabletop cutter to split any patterned tiles you are using into strips. You can vary the width of these, but where possible you want to get as much interesting detail onto each strip. Use nippers to break off different sized triangular pieces from each strip.

6 Place an inner row

Take the patterned triangles you have cut and start positioning them, with one side of the triangle placed against the inner border, and the "point" of the triangle facing outwards. Try to balance the design by eye, varying the size of the triangles, but keeping their positioning nice and even.

7 Establish the outer edge

Now, move onto the outer edge of the frame. Again, use "finished" edges of tiles to provide a neat outer surface. Split off the edges of the tiles you want to use using the cutter, then shape these into suitably sized triangular shapes with your nippers. With the inner and outer borders established, you can then fill in the space between. You will need to be patient to get a neat fit for irregular shapes – hold tile pieces over the gaps they must fill and mark your cut lines with a fibretip pen or chinagraph pencil.

8 Complete and grout

Grout the tiles carefully, being careful not to scratch or dull the surface of the mirror when cleaning off the grout. Use masking tape and paper to protect the mirror during this final step.

Project 5: Shell splashback

This project makes a splashback, which you can install behind a hand basin. You should use marine plywood for your backing board and finish the piece with a waterproof grout. Never use MDF in a damp environment as it will absorb water, swell and the mosaic pieces will become dislodged. It is also a good idea to use the concealed corner mount method (see page 197) to fix the completed splashback in place.

Tools

Pencil
Ruler
Fibretip pen
Nippers
Brush

Materials

Marine plywood
Paper
PVA
Waterproof glue
Vitreous tiles
Waterproof yacht varnish
Waterproof grout

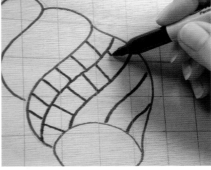

1 **Draw up the design using cut-outs**
Cut your board to size and draw a grid of squares the size of your tile squares – this provides a guide for the checkerboard background that is used in this piece. Create your shells with paper cut-outs – you can then position the shells using the grid as a guide. This allows you to create the design symmetrically, and also means that you can make minor adjustments to simplify the cutting of the background checkerboard.

2 **Create a tiling guide**
When you are happy with the positioning of the shells, draw their outlines onto the board, and transfer the detail within the outline shapes onto the board as well. Using a broad-tipped fibretip pen, darken all the lines of the shells and mark up the distinct tile bands.

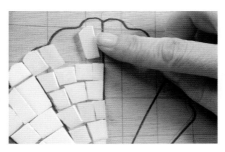 

3 Tile the shells first

The shells are tiled using a mixture of white and pearlescent tiles. Take care to fit the tiles to the bands you have drawn. For the triangular shapes within the scallop shells you need to carefully taper each tile piece so that it fits neatly into the allotted space. You will also need to cut the tiles so that each area is made up of symmetrically sized pieces. Work from the centre outwards on each tiling band, rather than from left to right, otherwise you may end up with tiny fragments as you complete each marked-up area.

4 Tile the background

Once all the shells are completed, begin tiling the checkerboard background. To get the tiles of the background to fit the outline of the shells you should first position each tile against the square grid, then mark areas that have to be cut away on the surface of the tile using a fibretip pen.

5 Ensure a waterproof finish

Finish the piece using a waterproof grout intended for use in bathrooms or other wet areas (check the label for suitability). Once the grout has dried, seal the edges and the back of the plywood with three coats of waterproof boat varnish.

6 Mount and seal

Mount the splashback onto the wall, using the concealed corner mount method (see page197). To ensure that no moisture penetrates behind the splashback once it is in place, seal the edges using a bead of waterproof silicone sealant. Give the finished piece a good polish to bring out the lustre of the pearlescent tiles.

Project 6: Clock

This clock has a circular, geometric design. The outer ring is quartered to represent the phases of the day: the brightness of the morning, the golden tones of the afternoon, the darkening dusk and the depth of the night. The inner ring mixes the colours of the outer ring in a busy radial pattern of thin split tiles and semicircular cuts. You can buy a clock-face and mechanism from a good craft store – otherwise, find a suitable cheap or old clock and dismantle it.

Tools
Long-armed compass
Electric jigsaw
Drill
Nippers
Paintbrush

Materials
MDF
Vitreous tiles
PVA
Clockface and mechanism
Grout
Paint
Keyhole plate

1 **Draw the circular outline of the clock**
The clock mechanism is mounted in a circular baseboard of MDF. Mark the centre of the circle clearly on the board then, using a long-armed compass, mark the outer edge of the clock.

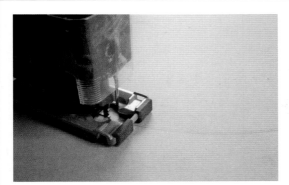

2 Cut the baseboard

Using an electric jigsaw, carefully cut out the circle you have drawn. (It is a good idea to practise following a curved line using a piece of waste wood first if this is the first time you have used a jigsaw.) Clamp or support the board as you cut it, stopping to reposition the board as you move around the circle.

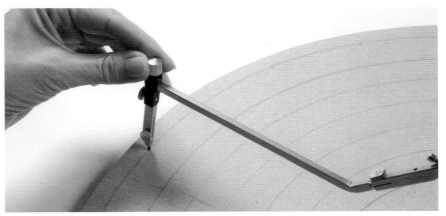

3 Draw tile guides

Now draw a circle slightly larger than the diameter of your clock-face, where the tiled area of the clock will begin. Work outwards, drawing progressively larger circles a "tile-and-grout" width apart – each of these rings will contain a row of tile pieces.

4 Cut an opening for the mechanism

Drill a hole at the centre of the circle and use this to hold the clock spindle so that you can draw around the outline shape of the clock mechanism. Then, use the hole you have drilled as the entry point for the jigsaw blade and run the saw around the outline you have drawn.

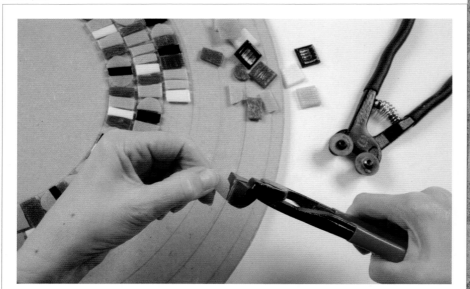

5 Begin cutting and laying tiles

Cut a stock of tiles before you start. The design is not fixed to a rigid grid of equally sized tiles, so you can vary the size and sequence of colours of the tile pieces as you choose. Here, the rectangular pieces are interspersed with semicircular pieces to add variety to the design. However, to fit each band of tiles into a circle you will need to taper the tile pieces slightly so that the end nearer the centre of the circle is slightly narrower than the end further away.

6 Fix the clock-face and mechanism

When the tiling is complete, let everything dry, and then apply grout. Clean up the tiles and then paint the central area of the baseboard with a colour that matches the tiles you have used. Finally, apply PVA glue to the baseboard, and then position the clock-face and mechanism, making sure that the numbers on the clock-face align correctly with the outer quadrants of tiles.

7 Mount the finished piece

Use a keyhole plate (see page 196) to hang the clock on the wall. If the clock mechanism you are using is thicker than the baseboard you can screw some blocks of MDF to the back of the baseboard so that the finished piece hangs level with the wall — the keyhole plate will need to be screwed to the topmost block.

Project 7: Leaf table

This design uses household tiles to create the surface of a small "occasional" table. However, the design could be enlarged to cover a larger tabletop, or the repeat of the leaf motif increased outwards in rings. Mosaic is well suited to tabletops because it provides a tough, heat-resistant finish that can easily be cleaned. However, it is advisable to seal the grout before you use the table as it is liable to stain, particularly if you spill coffee or fruit juice on it. This example uses a table kit from a specialist mosaic supplier – it has a routed surface with a lip around the edge that neatly protects the edges of the tiles. Alternatively, you can tile onto a circular piece of MDF, then use a metal or plastic strip as a "trim" around the edge of the tabletop, nailed or screwed into the side of the baseboard.

Tools
Fibretip pen
Tabletop tile cutter
Nippers
Paintbrush
Screwdriver

Materials
Paper
Table kit
Ceramic tiles
PVA
Waterproof grout
Varnish or furniture wax

1 Use cut-outs to draw up the design
Prepare the baseboard in the usual way – by sealing MDF with PVA. Draw up and cut out the main leaf motif, making several copies so that you can position the leaves evenly around the surface. When you are satisfied with their placement, carefully draw around each one using a thick pencil.

2 **Draw in the leaf stems**
Make a second cut-out for the shape of the leaf stem, then trace around this in the centre of each of the leaf shapes.

3 **Prepare your tile pieces**
Start to make tile pieces from household tiles by cutting each tile into evenly sized strips using a tabletop tile cutter.

4 **Shape the tile pieces**
Use tile nippers to cut each of the strips into spiky shapes for the leaf stems. Try to keep each piece fairly large so that this element of the leaf has a strong, linear feel.

5 Glue the stem pieces down

When everything looks good laid out on the board, start gluing, using a small paintbrush to apply waterproof PVA to the baseboard. Press your tile pieces into the glue and complete all the stem shapes and then leave the tiles to set.

6 Move onto the leaves

The leaves are completed using a similar "spiky" shatter fill, but with smaller pieces to give a busier effect. Work on one leaf at a time, completing it from the centre around the stems, and working outwards to the pencil outline. With shatter fills it is a good idea to cut a big stock of different shaped tiles so that you can try different combinations of pieces to get a neat fit. You will find you will need to use your nippers to make lots of adjustments by "nibbling" down tile edges.

7 Complete the background

The background is intended to deliberately contrast with the leaf motifs by using a soft monotone and laying the tiles in a traditional opus vermiculatum (see page 103) – where the fill is completed in uniform tile pieces that flow gently around the outlines of the shapes they contain.

8 Grout and finish

To give further uniformity to the background, a mid-grey grout is used which almost blends with the background colour. Once the grout is dry, clean up the tiles thoroughly, then assemble the table. Seal any bare wood using a suitable varnish or furniture wax. Use a water-based grout sealer on the mosaic surface, to protect the tabletop.

Project 8: Rose box

The wooden box used here was sold as a planter to hold a potted houseplant – hence the floral design. You could use any similar-sized wooden box for this purpose – you just need to place a plastic or ceramic tray inside to stand the pot on, otherwise the wood will soak up moisture from the pot. Alternatively you could use the box for an entirely different purpose – perhaps to hold pens and brushes, or kitchen utensils.

Tools

Tabletop tile cutter
Fibretip pen
Nippers
A range of paintbrushes
Domestic oven
Glue brush or spatula
Toothpicks

Materials

Ceramic tiles
Tile paints
Wooden box
PVA
Acrylic or emulsion paint
Grout
Clear varnish

The piece is a relief mosaic where the tiles stand out from the surface, rather than being inlaid, which is perhaps a more common way of combining mosaic with furniture or other household objects. Working in this way does require you to take considerable care with the edges of the tiled areas – so that the end result is attractive and also to ensure that no sharp edges are exposed. Here, household tiles were used, and each floral motif was finished with a continuous border cut from the glazed edges of tiles so that no unsightly edges of cut tile were left showing.

1 Pre-cut your tile pieces
First, make up flowers by cutting small rectangles of the different colours you want to use using a tabletop tile cutter. Mark the shapes with a fibretip pen before cutting to shape with tile nippers. If you haven't got the tile colours you want – very bright colours can be hard to find – then you can follow the guidance in the section on tile paints (see page 34) to prepare your own tiles in any colour you choose.

2 Paint the detail
Using tile paint applied with a thin artist's brush – you will need a really fine gauge such as a 00 or 000 brush – draw the detail of the flowers and leaves. Try to use clean, sweeping strokes to give a calligraphic quality to the drawing.

3 Outline each piece
The different pieces of the petals and leaves are each given a strong outline to give them more definition and interest. To add variety you can cut some large circles then paint a flower, bird or butterfly to position within the flower heads.

4 "Fire" the tiles
When everything is painted, "fire" the pieces in an ordinary domestic oven, following the tile paint manufacturer's instructions. When the pieces have cooled, assemble all the flowers on a piece of paper, moving them around until you are happy with the composition you have created. (It is a good idea to have made extra pieces so you can try different arrangements and get the whole piece to fit together neatly.)

5 Prime and seal the wood
Once you are satisfied with the composition, set aside the tiles, then prime all the surfaces of the box using some watered-down PVA to seal the wood – this will keep the tile glue from drying out too quickly as you lay the tiles.

6 Work on one side at a time

When the sealant coat has dried, begin transferring your pieces and gluing them down onto the surface of the box. When one flower motif is completed, cut small pieces from the tile edges to provide a neat border that snakes around the outside of the whole posy. Leave everything to dry thoroughly (and horizontally) – ideally overnight – before rotating the box and repeating the sequence of steps for the next "face".

7 Grout carefully

Once all the motifs are completed and thoroughly dried, start to grout. Remember that the edges are going to be visible, so work patiently on a small area at a time, and use pieces of kitchen towel or cloth to clean off excess grout from the tile surfaces and the surrounding wood as you work. Wooden toothpicks are useful for removing small pieces of excess grout from difficult corners.

8 Paint the finished box

When the grout has dried, apply a white undercoat and then paint a base colour over all the non-tiled surfaces. Paint carefully around the tiles – use a household emulsion as this can be cleaned off more easily than gloss or enamel paints.

9 Add detail and then varnish

Use a small brush to add polka dots – these might require a couple of coats to stand out from the background. Finally, apply a clear varnish to the painted areas and allow to dry.

9 Gallery

Gathered together on the following pages are some examples of contemporary mosaics which showcase the diversity of the art form, and the variety of approaches that different mosaic artists bring to the medium. The pieces are broadly grouped into categories and are intended to act as a resource and inspiration as you develop your own ideas and techniques.

▲*Solitude*
Irina Charny
Here a "trompe l'oeil" trick is employed so that the
figure appears to lean out in front of the frame that
supposedly surrounds her.

◀ *Portia*
Christine Brallier
The close cropping of the face makes this portrait compelling. The sinuous ribboning of the hair is important in giving the picture a smouldering energy.

▼*Astronomers*
Irina Charny
A mysterious image of looming figures with their heads rendered with pebbles. The earth colours of their clothes accentuate the blue sky shot through with multicoloured ribbons of stars.

▶ *Fish*
Jacqui Douglas
The cut out backing board emphasizes the bulbous shape of the fish, while the tiles are a clever mix of plain and patterned ceramic. The eye detail is a neat finishing touch.

▼*Tree of life*
Irina Charny
The hands are cut out to extend beyond and grasp the circumference of the globe. The sharp tonal gradation of the background around the base of the tree emphasizes the sense of the tree bursting into colourful life.

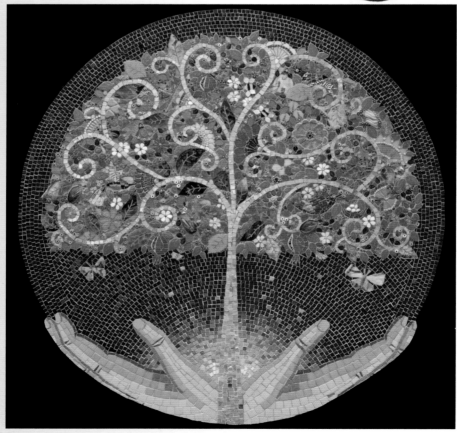

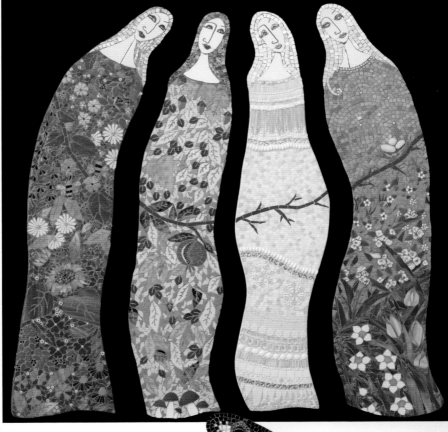

▲ Four seasons
Irina Charny
A beautiful use of cut-out shapes where
the separate figures, representing summer,
autumn, winter and spring are held together
by the delicate tendril of the same branch that
stretches horizontally across the mosaic, across
all four sections of the design illustrating the
seasonal changes.

▸ Colour Burst
Irina Charny
A beautiful cut-out design, with explosions of
blossoming and cascading colour. The black outline
gives an added richness and definition.

◄ *Onion pot and pedestal*
Caroline Kovacs
The strength of this three-dimensional piece comes from the simplicity of the white tiles combined with the elegant tracery of the grout lines. Colour is used only to accentuate the detail of the small irises around the column.

▶ *Liberace*
Kim Grant
These lucious, portly chickens are covered in a mixture of different glass and ceramic tiles, millefiori, and gold and silver leaf giving a rich, dense and highly tactile effect.

◀ *Mural*
Jacqui Douglas
Glass tiles, pebbles and ceramics
are combined in this piece to create
a strong, graphic image built upon
simple overlapping geometric shapes.

▶ *Flounder*
Kris Meigs
This strong design carefully balances a random fill
with the more formal cutting of the fish. The framing
border ties the design together, creating the effect
of a ceramic rug.

▼ *Splashback*
Kris Meigs
A bold and confident piece using large ceramic tiles
– the leaf design and muted colours work well with
the surrounding areas of wood.

◄ *Starry Night*
Caroline Kovacs
A confident
and successful
interpretation of
Vincent van Gogh's
famous painting.

▼*Irises*
Caroline Kovacs
These wonderful irises demonstrate that
to simplify a design to make a stunning
mosaic requires careful observation and
understanding of the subject.

▲*The Great Gate of Kiev*
Ilona Brustad
Contrasting background fills, a square grid in the lower third of the picture, a "shatter" fill for the sky —all are subtly used here to anchor and surround the strong golden form of the buildings.

Picture resource

If you are keen to start making mosaics but are not yet confident about producing your own design from scratch, we have provided some template pieces to get you started. A photograph of the finished mosaic is provided along with the grid and master drawing, which will allow you to recreate the design for yourself.

SCALE DRAWINGS

Each motif in this section is supplied with a gridded scale drawing for scaling up or down by hand, on a photocopier, or on a computer (see pages 114–123).

Sailboat

A simple design, which works nicely on a small scale to make a "miniature" picture. You could add further embellishment by adding a mosaic frame around the piece.

Seashells

Shell designs which evoke the sea are an ideal motif to use in bathrooms. This blue and white colour scheme adds freshness and light to a room.

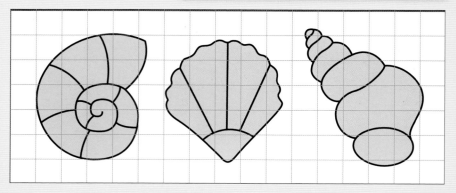

Angel fish

This is an easy piece to attempt with lots of possibilities for different use of colours and patterns. The shape is easy to draw and fill, and the results are effective with either a basic, bright set of colours or a deeper and more complex palette. The angel fish works well as a small decorative piece, or use as a large wall-sized mural in a bathroom.

Koi carp

A single fish outline is reused to provide all the shapes in the picture – both the fish and the shadows. This is a piece that would work well in a shower area or – if you are lucky enough to have one – on the bottom of a swimming pool! The drop shadow works particularly effectively when the piece is viewed under water.

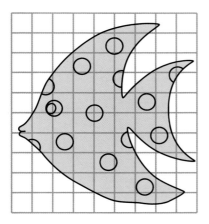

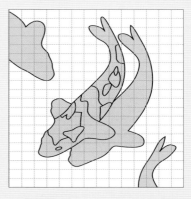

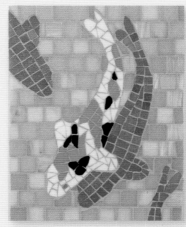

Elephant

A sweet little piece for a nursery wall panel because very young babies initially see things more clearly in black and white. You could use the same alternating, offset stripes to mosaic the outlines of different birds and animals. Remember when mounting pieces on the wall of a child's room to make sure it's securely fastened, and do not hang pieces directly over a bed.

Monkey clock

A humorous piece intended for a child's room. The key skill here is being able to cut out the shape using a jigsaw, and cutting a recess for the clock mechanism. Once that is done, the tiling is relatively simple – in this example ceramic tiles have been used. Take care around the perimeter, using pieces from the edge of tiles to give a neat finish. In this example "googly" eyes and diamantè stones have been added as further decoration – both can be easily obtained from craft shops.

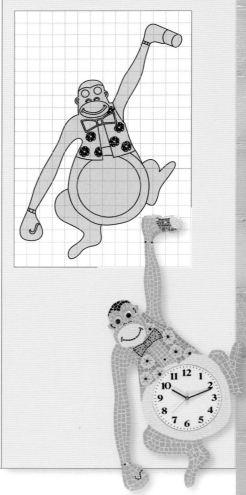

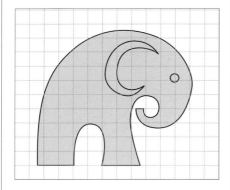

Steam engine

Very much a beginner's piece, this train is simple to draw and the design will not suffer if you are not completely accurate with the positioning of the tiles. If you can make all the wheels sit on a pencil line, the effect will be more grounded. Treat it as a fun piece to play with colours and develop your tile-cutting skills.

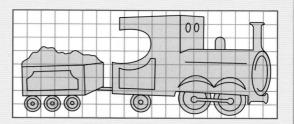

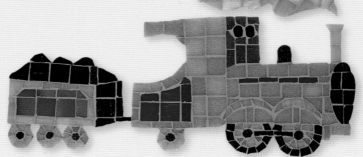

Love birds

A pretty decorative motif that you can adapt through extending or varying the patterns below the birds and by adding decorative materials, such as sequins or diamanté, as in this example. This is an ideal piece to make a plaque to commemorate a wedding or engagement, perhaps working in a date or adding the couple's names into the design.

Christmas tree

Use a jigsaw, cut the baseboard out of MDF about 5mm (¼ inch) beyond the outline of your drawing. You can then place eyelets and a picture wire on the back to hang the tree as a festive decoration in an entrance hall or stairwell. Dress the tree to your taste – create little parcels, candles, candy sticks or holly leaves. You could make the tree more natural and similar to a fir tree with straighter, pointed branches and add a trunk if you wish.

Heart trivet

This cutout design is used here to make a trivet but you could use a hidden keyhole mount to make this into a wall hanging. In this example you could also replace the inner circular tile at the bottom of the heart with a piece of mirror glass. If using ceramic tiles – as in this example – take care to cut pieces from the edges of tiles to use to create a smooth finish of uncut tiles around the perimeter of the heart.

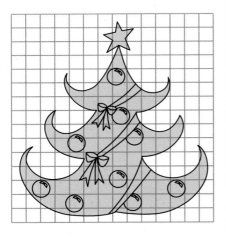

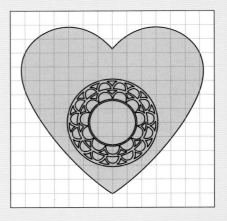

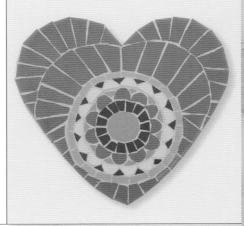

Apple

You can almost taste the crispness of this cut apple, in which the softness of the flesh is in contrast to the dark skin and the punctuation marks of the pips. Contouring the inner fill to the shape of the outline and core accentuates the sense of succulence.

Butterfly

The shape of the butterfly can be used and interpreted in so many ways. Here circular patterns have been used, working outwards from the centre and gradually filling the outline. In this example ceramic tiles have been used to give larger pieces and finer control of the shapes. If you want a more naturalistic butterfly, visit a library and look at books about these wonderful creatures to get inspiration from nature's colour and variety.

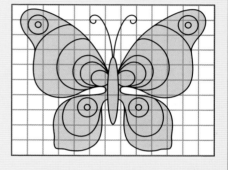

Swan

The shape of the swan – its elegance and simplicity – is defined by the smooth curve of its neck, so take time to get the drawing of the outline of the bird absolutely right. Then take similar care with your tiling, making sure that the tiles taper neatly and form a continuous smooth curving outline.

Toucan

The toucan's stark plumage and powerful, colourful beak make it instantly recognizable. This "over the shoulder" pose makes for a denser design. Work outwards from the eye and the beak first – positioning the smaller pieces of mosaic required for these details is easier on an empty surface, rather than trying to fit them in later. In this example the plumage has been realized using contrasting black and white tiles with a few mid tones. You could experiment with blues and bottle greens.

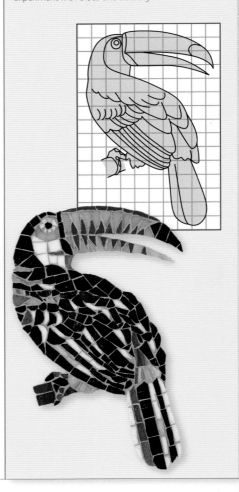

Dove

This design is a very graphic interpretation of a bird, but as the finished example shows, you could use very different tilings and colour schemes to produce quite different effects. The motif also works at different scales, as a tile-sized piece or as a large picture.

Macaw

Although the softness of feathers is the very opposite of the hard-edged feel of ceramic tiles, mosaic actually works very well in rendering the sense of a bird, like this scarlet macaw. Use the brightest tiles to give the vibrant sense of the bird's plumage – you can follow a naturalistic design, or, if you prefer, take liberties and experiment with more raucous colour combinations. Pay most attention to the face of the bird where the tiles give a sense of the mechanical strength of the beak.

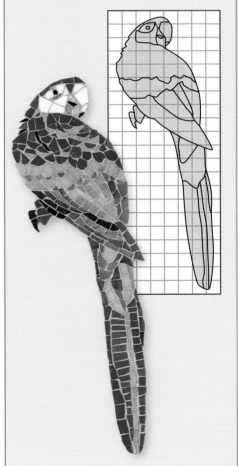

Retro flowers

The example of this design created for this book works on quite a small scale, however, it is a design that could be scaled up to work successfully as a mural-sized piece. As an alternative to the brown and orange colour scheme an equally retro effect can be created using cooler blues and greens.

Cactus

This design is best executed in ceramic tiles, not only because the larger pieces allow you to make bigger "spiky" shapes, but also because you can combine patterned tiles to add interest. Here, a thin line within a patterned tile has been cut out to use as outline tiles around the cactus plant, while the border framing the piece is cut from similar sections of a different design. Before embarking on this, you need to make sure you have a sufficient stock of patterned tiles to provide the quantity of tile pieces you will need.

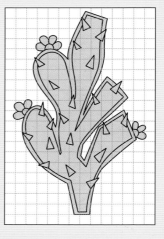

Sunflowers

Sunflowers, with their densely packed, shaggy petals and seed-laden centres, are instantly recognizable. This motif works well on a large scale, matching the size of the real plant, perhaps as a wall mural or as a tall, thin panel.

Leaf table

This tabletop design is a very simple repeat of a leaf motif. Use evenly spaced cutouts to fill your shape – here a circle, but repeating templates can be easily extended to fill out a rectangular or square area.

Arrow frame

This geometric frame is an adaptable design, because the repeat pattern is simple and does not require the overall dimensions of the frame to be square – you can "stretch" the design in either direction by adding additional arrow sections. However, you do need to be confident cutting triangles, and you will find that to fit the grid, the triangular pieces need to be cut down to provide the necessary space for the diagonal grout line.

Large Celtic knot

An ancient motif, often seen in jewellery and other decorative crafts. The symmetry of the piece makes it ideal for inclusion in a mosaiced tabletop. Celtic designs are generally rendered in greens and reds to achieve a traditional look. However, a modern, abstract effect can be achieved by using a more vivid colour palette.

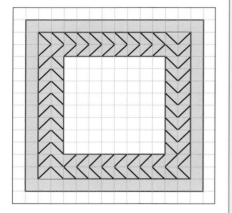

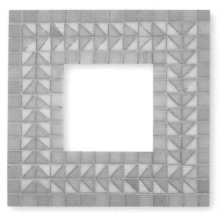

Moorish design

This design has a strong Middle Eastern feeling, enhanced by the use of a "hot" colour palette. Geometric designs look even stronger when repeated. This design works well repeated as a horizontal border – perhaps within a tiled splashback, or repeated across a table top, it makes a stunning surface for an outdoor patio table. You need to be confident in cutting accurate triangles because the grout lines will expose any inconsistencies, particularly in the black tiles.

Paisley

The classic Paisley design is a droplet-shaped motif that originates in the Indian sub-continent, but takes its name from the Scottish town whose weavers adapted the design in the nineteenth century. The design is built up with concentric shapes, working from the inside outwards, this version is fairly complex, with radiating droplets. It is well suited to being used as the centrepiece of a design.

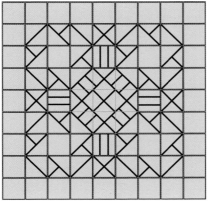

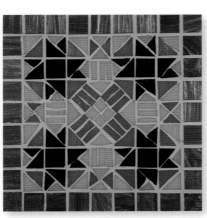

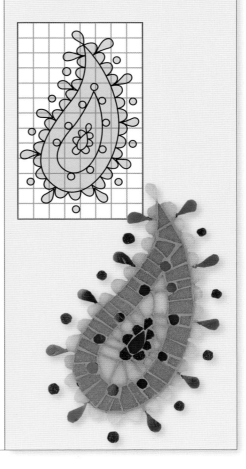

Glossary

Andamenti These are the lines along which mosaic tiles are laid, the lines of coursing of the mosaic.

Ceramic tiles Ceramic tiles are made from thin layers of fired clay. They are a popular mosaic material on account of the wide range of colours available and the fact that many types of tile can be easily cut and shaped with standard tools, such as tile cutters and tile nippers.

Grout The cement which fills the gaps between tiles. Grouting refers to the process of applying grout to a mosaic.

Laying To lay is to put the individual tiles of a mosaic in place.

Millefiori Literally "thousand flowers" in Italian, this term refers to small tesserae created by the fusion of many glass rods arranged so that the cross section creates a flower pattern. These rods are then sliced thinly and encased in glass.

Mounting To mount a mosaic is to set it in its final location.

Opus This is the Latin word for work. The plural is "opera".

Opus musivum This is an effect rather like ripples on a pond, with repeated rows of tesserae spreading out to fill a background to the edges of the mosaic area.

Opus paladanium A random-like, crazy-paving effect of placement of irregular mosaic tesserae.

Opus regulatum As the name suggests, this is a very regular pattern of tesserae, like bricks in a wall, or squares on a chessboard.

Opus sectile This is a technique where, instead of being made up of lots of individual tesserae, shapes in a picture are made from larger, specially cut, pieces (perhaps of tile or stone).

Opus verniculatum A single row, or several rows, of tesserae following the outline of a feature (such as a figure or other subject) in a mosaic. The effect is a little like a halo, highlighting the subject and providing contrast against a background with tesserae laid in a different style. "Vermiculatum" means "wormlike" and is so called because it curves around the contours of the design.

Smalti Enamelled glass of the kind used in Byzantine mosaics.

Squeegee A tool for spreading grout. The squeegee has a rubber blade on one edge which helps force the grout into all the spaces.

Tabletop tile cutter A tool specifically designed for cutting ceramic tiles, although it can sometimes cut other materials such as glass. The cutting process has two stages. A thin blade (typically a cutting wheel) is drawn across the surface, making a small straight score mark in the glaze. Then pressure is applied evenly on either side of this line to snap the tile along the line.

Tesserae These are the components of a mosaic, which may include cut and uncut tiles, pebbles, and found objects.

Tile nippers A handheld tool for breaking and snipping mosaic materials such as vitreous glass tiles, ceramic tiles or crockery.

Vitreous glass Square mosaic tiles made in moulds from glass paste. They have a smooth top and a rough, textured back.

Resources

UK

■ **Edgar Udney & Co Ltd**
The Mosaic Centre
314 Balham High Road
London SW17 7AA
Tel: +44 20 8767 8181

■ **Focus Ceramics**
Unit 4 Hamm Moor Lane
Weybridge Trading Estate
Weybridge
Surrey KT15 2SD
Tel: +44 1932 854881
www.focusceramics.com

■ **Mosaic Workshop**
Unit B
443–449 Holloway Road
London N7 6LJ
Tel: +44 20 7272 2446
www.mosaicworkshop.com

■ **Reed Harris Ltd**
Riverside House
27 Carnwath Road
London SW6 6JE
Tel: +44 20 7736 7511
www.reed-harris.co.uk

■ **Tower Ceramics**
91 Parkway
Camden Town
London NW1 9PP
Tel: +44 20 7485 7192
www.towerceramics.co.uk

USA

■ **Artful Crafter, Inc.**
741 Lawson Avenue
Havertown, PA 19083
Tel: +1 877 321 2080
www.artfulcrafter.com

D&L Stained Glass Supply, Inc
1440 W. 52nd Avenue
Denver, CO 80221
Tel: +1 800 525 0940
www.dlstainedglass.com

Delphi Stained Glass
3380 East Jolly Road
Lansing, MI 48910
Tel: +1 800 248 2048
www.delphiglass.com

Dick Blick Art Materials
P.O. Box 1267
Galesburg, IL 61402-1267
Tel: +1 800 723 2787
www.dickblick.com

Glass Crafters Stained Glass, Inc
398 Interstate Court
Sarasota, FL 34240
Tel: +1 941 379 8333
www.glasscrafters.com

Happycraftn's Mosaic Supplies
28244 Essex Avenue
Tomah, WI 54660
Tel: +1 608 372 3816
www.happycraftnsmosaicsupplies.com

Mosaic Mercantile
P.O. Box 78206
San Francisco, CA 94107
Tel: +1 877 966 7242
www.mosaicmercantile.com

CANADA

Interstyle Ceramic & Glass Ltd
3625 Brighton Avenue
Burnaby, Vancouver
V5A 3H5
Tel: +1 604 421 7229
www.interstyle.ca

AUSTRALIA

Flat Earth TileWorks
4 Forth Street
Kempsey, NSW 2440
Tel: +61 2 6562 8327
www.midcoast.com.au/~vanz/

Metric Tile
38–42 Westall Road
Springvale, VIC 3171
Tel: +61 3 9547 7633
www.infotile.com.au/metrictile

Mosaria
311 Colburn Ave
Victoria Point,
QLD 4165
Tel: +61 7 3207 6380
www.mosaria.com

Index

Credits

Quarto would like to thank the following artists for kindly supplying images for inclusion in this book:

(Key: t top, b bottom)

Christine Brallier www.cbmosaics.com page 229t
Ilona Brustad www.ilonabrustad.com page 235
Irina Chary www.icmosaics.com: pages 228, 229b, 230b, 231,
Jacqui Douglas pages 230t, 233b
Kim Grant www.kimgrantmosaics.com page 232b,
Caroline Kovacs pages 232t, 234
Sue Majewski www.artsandscraps.org page 89b
Kris Meigs www.meigsart.com page 233

All other images are the copyright of Quarto Publishing plc. While every effort has been made to credit contributors, Quarto would like to apologize should there have been any omissions or errors – and would be pleased to make the appropriate correction for future editions of the book.